I0830198

# THE CRIMINAL JUSTICE SYSTEM WITH A VIEW FROM THE BOTTOM

By **Joseph A. Marro**

Copyright 2013 by Joseph A. Marro
All rights reserved

No part of this book may be reproduced in any format
without written permission from the author and the
publisher.

E. B. Alston
1112 Rogers Road
Graham, NC 27253

http://alstonbooks.xyz/

December 2018

Printed and bound in the United States of America

Cover drawing "The Weight of Time" by Al Sailer
Cover design by Barbara Alston

Library of Congress Control Number
2013933853

ISBN: **9781792732737**
The Criminal Justice System
with a View from the Bottom
By Joseph A. Marro

# Acknowledgments

In recognition of all those in the criminal justice system who assist in so many ways.

My thanks to Zeletta A. Sailer for her kind permission to include Al Sailer's manuscript and some of his drawings in this memoir.

Appreciation is given to Gerry Oliver, who took an interest in Al's drawings and wrote about him for the Delaware County Daily Times.

My appreciation to the writing group at the Central Orange Senior Center, Hillsborough, NC, for their suggestions while I developed this memoir.

Thanks to Annette Hubbard for her kind assistance in typing the manuscript.

And lastly, my thanks to my editor Rita Berman whose suggestions and guidance I could not have done without.

Joseph A. Marro

# Table of Contents

# THE CRIMINAL JUSTICE SYSTEM

I retired from the criminal justice system in 1977, after 23 years of dealing with the criminal element of society as a United States Probation/Parole Officer.  Each day was different from the last as I worked with a wide range of personalities, among them probationers, parolees, prisoners, lawyers and even judges.  Everybody's life has some trials and tribulations, but most of us don't allow these to control our behavior or affect our well being.  Unfortunately, for Al Sailer and others, they failed to overcome such setbacks in spite of the help offered by the Federal Justice System.  In Al's case he spent a total of 26 years in various penal institutions before he learned how to manage his life outside of prison walls.

After my retirement at the young age of 52, I found employment in a different field as an assistant to the Purchasing Director of a brewery.  However, my experiences as a probation/parole officer are unforgettable and I feel it may benefit others if I write about my interactions with those individuals who broke the law, and whose cases were assigned to me.[1]

Al Sailer's story is particularly heartrending for he was an intelligent and extremely talented self taught artist as revealed in his manuscript and drawings that are included in the Appendix.  In order to present Al's story, I must first give mine.

I was about 7 or 8 years of age when my uncle asked, "What do you want to be when you grow up?"  I answered, "I want to be a cop."  My uncle wanted to know "Why?", and I answered, "So I can lock up my Dad!"

---

[1] The names of all cases mentioned have been changed, except for Al Sailer whose manuscript is included in the Appendix.

My sister and I were reared in a tightly controlled atmosphere, and when our father told us to sit on the front step, we knew that was an order punishable by unpleasantness if violated.  We were both good, well-behaved children but my father set rules that had to be obeyed without questions, My mother was also a disciplinarian and I recall two occasions when I was beaten by her with a "cat of nine tails" (a rod that held several long thin strips of leather); once when I ate most of the figs from the fig tree growing in the back yard, and the other time was when I watched a lighted match burn.  I was fascinated by the dancing flame and I dripped it on the paper covered kitchen floor that my mother had just mopped.  The welts on my back were later seen by my maternal grandmother who asked who put them there; of course I told her, and after that the "cat of nine tails" disappeared.

My father worked in a shoe factory and my mother worked in a paper box factory, with her meager wage being supplemented by waitressing jobs.  My father's job had frequent layoffs and he worked for a period with the Works Progress Administration as a laborer, and on occasion, we received food stamps from the welfare program.  I remember going to the grocery store with a food stamp and getting a bag of potatoes which was our supper that night. Other days, we bought day old bread and my paternal grandmother, with whom we were living, would sprinkle olive oil on the slices along with herbs from a back yard garden and then toast them in the coal fired oven; that would be our supper that night.  Other meals consisted of fried blossoms from a plant growing in the rear garden; this was a treat since they tasted like scrambled eggs.  In spite of this diet, we all enjoyed good health.  I recall being given a nickel for lunch when I was in the 9th grade and that bought me a satisfying lunch of two miniature pretzels and a small chocolate bar.

On the rare occasion when one of us felt ill, a telephone call from a nearby store brought the physician to our home carrying his little black bag, and after examination and description of symptoms, he would leave medication with instructions, and be satisfied with a minimum fee.

Unfortunately, there was frequent discord in the family home due mainly to my father's drinking problems. Once, when I was about 6 years of age, he put his fist through the parlor wall in a fit of rage, and on another occasion, he reached into the bird cage where my mother had two parakeets and after grabbing one my father ended up on the floor in a drunken stupor with the dead bird clutched in his clenched fist. There were many embarrassing incidents that neighbors saw and ignored, such as the night he came home from the bar and threw our two wooden rocking chairs off the front porch. Sometimes I had to go to the neighborhood bar to assist him home and then help him get undressed and into bed. The next morning, he and my mother would argue and occasionally he would get physical. When I saw this I would jump between then to stop any battering. When I got older I realized my mother may well have contributed to some of their arguments. The situation never improved and my sister and I became teenagers who had endured constant turmoil.

Another incident took place when I was about 7 years of age. At the time, we were living in my paternal grandmother's three story home at 1915 S. 11th Street, and summer time activities were spent at the local school yard. I liked to play marbles where each person puts a certain number of marbles in a circle and the participants take turns "shooting" with their favorite marble with the aim to knock as many marbles out of the circle as possible.  Marbles that were knocked out of the circle's limits became the property of the shooter.  When you missed knocking any out of the circle, it was the next person's turn to shoot.  Well, on this particular day, after losing all my marbles I returned home feeling very sad.  My sister, who was two years older than me, asked, "What happened to your marbles?"  I responded that I had lost them.  "How did you lose them?" she asked.  When I told her another kid knocked them out of the circle, she immediately marched me back to the school yard and asked me to point out the kid.  She walked directly over to him, faced him and demanded that he return the marbles to me immediately.  Now he really won those marbles fair and square but he gave them back meekly.  My sister proudly marched me back home along with my new supply of marbles.

I was about 12 years of age when my mother asked me if I wanted to play an instrument, and I expressed an interest in a clarinet.  We went to the Wurlitzer music store at 11$^{th}$ and Chestnut Sts., but clarinets were beyond my mother's means.  However, a trumpet was on sale for $l2.88 with six free lessons so she bought that instead.   Well, never having had or played a bugle, it took two lessons before I learned how to get a sound out of that horn.  My mother hired a private teacher from the Strawberry Mansion area, it was a great distance from our home, and he used public transportation to get to our location.  He needed the job and paid the trolley fare out of the $2.00 lesson fee.  My mother scraped that amount from the family's meager income.

I became efficient enough with that horn to enroll in the high school band, but after only the second day at school for rehearsal; my trumpet was stolen from the science lab where I was studying.  When the Principal, Frank

C. Neiweg, learned of this theft, he arranged for me to acquire a trumpet through school funds from a local music shop in South Philadelphia. The Music department Director, Jay Speck, was not in favor of the purchase but Mr. Neiweg's decision prevailed. By the time I got the second trumpet the brass section of the orchestra was filled and so I lost the opportunity to be a part of the band.

I stopped attending high school at the start of 12B (the second half of my senior year), because I intended to enlist in the U.S. Navy. A friend and I, both 17 at the time, decided we would join the submarine division. My mother refused to sign my enlistment papers, though my friend's mother signed his and he left town. The principal sent for my mother and urged that she try to convince me to remain in school, but she responded that she had already done that and I refused. My cousin had been serving on the Light Cruiser, the USS Vincennes in the Coral Sea, and died when the ship was bombed by a Japanese aircraft. I planned to be his avenger.

Because my mother refused to allow me to sail away, I sought and secured a job working at the Philadelphia Naval Base as an Apprentice Ship fitter. I worked on the battleship USS New Jersey and watched its launch on December 7, 1942. I remained in this job until my 18th birthday when I visited my local draft board to register for the draft. I replaced one of the married registrants and was given a date to report to the Naval Recruiting Station. The doctor who gave me the physical exam was my own personal physician, and he expressed concern that I had chosen not to finish my high school education.

Within a matter of weeks, I was shipped to the Naval Training Station in Sampson, N.Y. for boot camp which lasted 8 weeks paying me $66.00 per month as a Apprentice Seaman. I was next sent to the US Naval

Training Center at Navy Pier in Chicago, Ill., for training as an Aviation Metalsmith.  I enjoyed my time in Chicago because servicemen were welcomed by the residents who couldn't seem to do enough to express their thanks to us. We received invitations to join their families for dinner and some people even sent gifts to our parents to show their appreciation for our serving.

At the time I enlisted, my Mother was living alone as my father had left the family home about 2 years earlier. Because of her limited income, I chose to have an allotment withdrawn from my monthly earnings to assist her.  I had relatively few expenses myself and for entertainment there was the USO which was free.  The training course in Chicago lasted about 9 months, and with a rating of seaman 1C, I was shipped to the University of the Air, in Corpus Christi, Texas.  There I earned a rating of AM3C being paid $78.00 monthly.  My job as a metalsmith was to check every aspect of the planes exterior to be certain there were no evidences of cracks or other damages, and if found, repairs were made.

One morning, I was called to the office of the commanding Officer a short, stocky, red faced, stern looking man. He showed me a drinking glass with a picture of a fully dressed gal on the outside of the glass, but she was nude on the inside of the glass.  He asked if I could duplicate that drawing, obviously aware from my personnel file that I attended the Philadelphia Museum School of Art on a scholarship granted during my Junior High School days.  I replied that I could and he said I would be assigned a special rating and would be painting the squadron emblem on all the station's aircraft.  I respectfully declined explaining that I was already learning a trade that I hoped to use when discharged, and he replied angrily, "If you refuse this assignment you'll never make another rating increase while

I'm in command of this station." Not wanting to give up the training I had already received, I decided to stand my ground and not give in to his ultimatum.

I left his office disappointed fearing I was destined to remain a 3rd class petty officer. But on the off chance maybe I still might be upgraded when the required interval had passed, I took the test for 2nd class. Happily, I made it and my pay was increased to $96.00 monthly. Several months later I took the test for 1st class and I made that as well and was raised to $114.00 per month.

In my position, I was required to fly in any airplane I worked on and that entitled me to "flight skins", which resulted in a 50% increase in monthly pay. Some of the other sailors, metalsmiths or mechanics, who expressed a fear of flying, asked those of us who enjoyed flying, to stand in for them. We received no additional pay, we just enjoyed being aloft.

Around August 1945, I was listed for transfer to San Diego, California, finally being granted my wish to be shipped overseas, but Japan surrendered on August 15th and the war having ended, my transfer order was rescinded and I was eventually transferred to the Naval Station at Bainbridge, Md. to be processed for an honorable discharge. I attempted to re-enlist but was told my rank would be reduced to 3rd class petty officer so I accepted the discharge on April 30, 1946. Weeks later, I visited the recruiting station in Philadelphia and was told again that I could only expect the 3rd class rating, so I gave up a career in the Navy.

Having sent no word to my mother that I was being discharged, I called her to say that I was in Philly and on my way home. I hailed a taxi and within minutes I was standing in front of our home being hugged and welcomed by the few neighbors who were present.  That was a happy memory.

I soon learned that the allotment checks that were sent home each month were in a bank account in my name.  So one of the first things I did was to locate and buy a suitable home so there would be no more renting.  I found a place on a main street, a large three bedroom row home which had great possibilities.  Eventually, I remodeled the entire property and put the deed in my mother's name.

Soon after my return home, I enrolled in a program under the GI Bill, that had been established to educate returning veterans,  and I was able to complete my high school education and receive my diploma.  I then took the exam for college entrance, earned an appropriate score and was enrolled in a new junior college program at Rittenhouse Area college, established for the overflow of returning veterans.

After completing the two-year course, I was accepted as a sophomore at Temple University.  While stationed in Corpus Christi, Texas, I had enrolled as a student at Texas A&M, and pursued basic courses in Psychology.  I had falsely said I was a high school graduate and that I wrote to the high school asking that my transcript be forwarded to them.

At Temple University, I received credit for the two Psychology courses I had completed, with the 6 semester hours being credited toward my double major in Psychology/Sociology and I earned a BA Degree in 1952. (Nine years later, I pursued a Graduate Degree in Group Dynamics).

Upon graduation, I filed numerous applications for employment with various state agencies.  The first response came from the Pennsylvania Department of Public Assistance, advising me that my score placed me on a eligibility list, and at a subsequent interview, I was hired and appointed as a Senior Visitor (caseworker), to cover a transient district in central Philadelphia. Duties were to visit recipients of welfare to determine their continued eligibility for financial aid. Initially, the job was an acceptable one despite having to visit homes infested with vermin, and very unclean conditions.

One of these properties was a large rooming house at 6th St, and Girard Avenue, where I had to meet with the manager of the facility in order to confirm the residence of one of the clients in my caseload. The manager, a large, obese woman, answered my questions while she lay in her bed in a  prone position. While I interviewed her, roaches crawled over her body but she seemed oblivious to them. Not wanting to carry any of these roaches or their eggs home with me, I kept moving and tapping my feet to discourage them from getting attached to me. I left the room quickly after receiving the necessary information on my client, who it turned out, was living in another room in this building.

It's been about 60 years since my visit to that client, but I recall it vividly, and remember it clearly as if it occurred yesterday. The client, Mary Daley, was a 50 year old female, single, who was obviously intoxicated. I introduced myself and explaining the reason for my visit asked how she was getting along. She responded by demanding, "Don't you know what's wrong with me?" She then lifted her dress and with a suction sound, pulled off the colostomy bag attached to her right side. The odor of the alcohol and the nasty odor coming from the bag now filtering in the air was overwhelming, but I managed to stay to complete the interviews. I was certainly happy to leave her room and eventually I found another job that was more satisfying.

One good aspect of that job, an unexpected benefit was I met the clerical staff supervisor, a most attractive and intelligent woman, who later became my wife.

After the visit to that rooming house, I felt there had to be more pleasant and rewarding work for me, so I took a gamble and resigned. I felt confident that I would have no trouble finding a new position. I read the local want ads and saw there was an opening at the Kaiser Metal Products Co., in Bristol, PA, for a sheet metal worker. After an interview and a physical exam, I was hired, but after that first day, I realized the two hour driving time each way plus the ten workday was more than I wanted, so I resigned. A couple of weeks later, I was accepted as an Outside Machinist at the Westinghouse Electric Turbine Division in Lester, PA. I held this job for a year until it ended due to contract fulfillment. So I was laid off and again onto a new job search.

It was while I was working for Westinghouse that I married my wife, the clerical staff supervisor, after an 18-month courtship. We were married on September 11, 1954, and our honeymoon was a trip through the northeastern states to Niagara Falls, in a 1948 Dodge that I had purchased upon graduation from college. It was a great vehicle, sturdy as a tank with a heavy metal body, and its comfort made our trip most enjoyable.

My wife, Ann, was a very attractive, intelligent person, and I found her to be a kind, considerate, warm and caring. We became engaged around the Christmas holiday in 1953, at the Latin Casino which was a night club located in Philadelphia at the time. I often think back to that evening when a notable piano playing bandleader, Al Morgan, was featured and I regret that I failed to ask him to play a tune for my wife to be. She would not have sought such attention, but I feel it would have given her a deserved moment in the limelight.  She liked to have me accompany her to the dress salon when she selected her trousseau and sought my approval on whatever dresses she modeled.  I felt that everything actually accented her beauty.

It was shortly after our return from our honeymoon, that I received notice from the Pennsylvania Board of Parole informing me that an opening prevailed and I could arrange for an interview at the Philadelphia office.  I applied immediately and after a brief interview with the Chief Parole Officer he approved my application and arranged an appointment for me with Major Henry Hill, the Chairman of the Board in Harrisburg, PA.  Later, at the Harrisburg interview, I was hired and assigned to the Philadelphia district.  I soon realized that this line of work was my destiny.  I enjoyed the work, and developed a good relationship with my co-workers as well as the caseload I was assigned to supervise.

During the early weeks of this employment, I had to arrest a young fellow (no more than 20 years of age), for violating his probation.  It was a minor violation and as this was my first experience of dealing with an offender who might be committed to prison, my supervisor handled the interview and ultimately recommended that the violator (who had never served any prison time and who was crying at the time), be continued on probation with a warning.  The young man was much relieved.

It wasn't long before I was a seasoned Probation/Parole Officer in full charge of my caseload, and I lost some of the empathy I felt at that initial experience. Still, when I had to take into custody another member of my caseload, because he had married without first securing permission (one of the rules of the system that was later changed), I went to his home and he had just returned from work. I gave him the choice of riding with me to the county prison or be picked up by a police vehicle.  If I didn't know the offender well enough, I would not have allowed a choice, especially as I was alone.  If there was ever any suspicion of possible problems with a parolee, I knew an arrest should be made with a partner or with police assistance.  He chose to ride with me, and after he showered, shaved and changed clothes, we proceeded to the local prison.  At a violation hearing two days later, he was released and returned to the community.

On another one occasion I had to arrest a violator who was 6' 4" and must have weighed over 225 pounds.  In that instance, I had a fellow officer accompany me.  We found the man at his place of employment, working in a meat locker hanging sides of beef.  He gave us no trouble, came along willingly which was good because we couldn't even handcuff him, his wrists were so big.

Once, when I was Duty Officer of the Day, a call came in that a probationer had barricaded his home preventing his family from gaining entrance.  As the duty officer I was required to respond, with a fellow officer we arrived at the home and saw that both the front and rear entrances were blocked with furniture.  However, we were able to gain entrance by climbing through a rear unlocked window, and as we moved quietly through the house we threw whatever could be used as a weapon out of the rear window.  Eventually we wound up on the second floor and found the subject of interest in a bedroom sound asleep. We took him into custody without a struggle, handcuffed him and transported him to the county prison.

Toby Grant was a slightly built fellow in his early 20s, who was reporting as required, visited me around the Christmas season.  While on probation for robbery he entered my office and wished me a "Merry Christmas" as he pulled a pair of black leather gloves from his inside his jacket and said, "Here's a gift for you."   I said, "We don't accept gifts," and he responded, "But I just picked them up for you at Gimbels."   I thanked him for his thought and told him he could return them to Gimbels in the same manner he acquired them, as his "generosity" could be interpreted as a violation. He left my office smiling.

Another case of interest was that of Charles Haney who had been sentenced to life in prison for murder.  H had returned from work one day, earlier than expected, and found his wife in bed with a neighbor. He killed them both with shots from a 12 gauge shotgun, then he reloaded, placed the shotgun under his chin and blew half his face away.  Hospitalized for some time, he was eventually sentenced to serve his life term which was commuted to 15 years.  He was released on parole after 10 years.

After being a State Parole Agent for about 3 years, I learned of an opening with the Federal system as a U.S. Probation/Parole Officer.  I submitted an application and was soon called for an interview before two Federal judges. They both were stern, unsmiling individuals, and their demeanor increased my apprehension of appearing before such highly seated members of the of the justice system. However, I pulled myself together by recalling the advice given me by my supervisor at the State Parole Board, who had said, "Just remember, they put their pants on the same way you do."

I felt that the interview went well; I thanked them for the opportunity and in turning to exit the room, I tripped over the carpeting and almost fell.  Now I was embarrassed but as I turned toward the judges, I noticed a slight smile on their faces and that comforted me.

Two weeks later I received a letter of appointment from the Administrative Office in Washington, D.C. and I started my career as a U.S. Probation/Parole Officer.  In this position, I represented the U.S. District Court, the U.S. Bureau of Prisons and the four U.S. military branches. This job entailed my doing pre-sentence investigations on defendants who committed Federal crimes. On the basis of the circumstances of the offense, along with the findings of the life of the defendant from the time of his/her birth to the commission of the offense, I would make a recommendation as to what sentence should be imposed, either probation or a prison term. Of course, the judge would make that determination.

At least once every two weeks, I was required as a duty officer to be present in the courtroom at the hearings of several offenders listed for sentencing that day, in case the judge had any question about the cases appearing before him. The presiding judge this day was one who demanded absolute silence in his courtroom. The cases to be sentenced that day were not unusual in any way except for the fact that this particular judge would not tolerate any distractions. The individual about to be sentenced would be called to stand before the bench, the U.S. attorney and defense counsel would make their statements, and I, seated at a table adjacent to the judge's bench, would make notes that I felt could be of importance. It happened that my pencil made a scratching noise as it glided across the paper tablet and I saw the judge cast a severe glare at me, causing me to drop the pencil and stop taking notes. Shades of my father! That glare, that piecing look was as demanding as words unsaid. It brought back memories of my father and the obedience he so ingrained in me during my childhood.

During the course of this employment, I met some very interesting people. Occasionally, I dealt with certain defendants who felt they could buy their way out of potentially severe penalties, but they soon learned this did not happen in the Federal system.  Once, after an initial interview with an offender at his home, he stuffed a $100.00 bill in my jacket pocket suggesting I enjoy my lunch.  I withdrew the bill and placed it on the mantelpiece and politely said it wasn't necessary as I didn't eat lunch.

Another time, when I was interviewing the father of an offender, he offered to pay my home mortgage if I could help his son.  Of course I declined, but I felt I had to report this offer to the court, but the judge construed this offer merely as the concern of an interested parent, rather than a bribe and of no real significance.  This well know father was a  former federal offender who had served several years in custody, was now in a prominent position in the community and was just  trying to protect his son from serious consequences that could/would affect his future.

During my early years in this job, I was one of several officers touring certain Federal prisons and on this occasion, we visited a juvenile institution in West Virginia.  The inmates of this prison were between the ages of 18 and 21, and most were serving indeterminate sentences.  Depending on their adjustment in the institution, they could be released on parole upon approval of a parole hearing committee.

After a general tour of the facility, I was able to see that there was little supervision or training of these juveniles, enabling them to congregate in small groups if they chose to do so.  Later, I sat in on three parole hearings scheduled for that afternoon and I observed the process. After the hearings were completed, one of the committee members asked me what I thought of the institution and I answered, in my usual honest, forthright manner, namely that I felt there was an apparent lack of supervision, that it appeared to be a warehousing operation with offenders being able to congregate and most likely learn more unacceptable behavior, getting useful tips from their fellow offenders.

Well, that committee member appeared visibly upset by my comment and I soon learned that he was the main force behind the establishment of the facility. Somehow, I felt the detriment of my comment for a couple of years afterward as possible opportunities evaded me without sound reason.

I recall being the pre-sentence writer on the case of a realtor who unlawfully approved mortgage applications and when at his sentencing hearing before a newly appointed judge, the defendant referred to me as "Joe", leading the judge to think that there was some inappropriate familiarity between me and the defendant. Although the Chief U.S. Probation Officer defended me, indicating that this happened frequently, that there was nothing of significance in a first name reference by many defendants, I was always able to note that this particular judge's attitude toward me was affected by that one reference. (Strange how just one simple incident, though meaningless, may have a long lasting effect on a person's judgment of another).

During my years with the Federal Justice system, I dealt with many defendants who were well known professionals, some famous, some infamous (Rocky Graziano, Frank "Blinky" Palermo and others), and I also became acquainted with some influential lawyers and politicians. There were potential benefits to these associations but more importantly, risks. I quickly learned that despite the attorneys' well regarded reputation, some were sly, devious manipulators.

An incident that almost cost me my job, involved a well known, influential Media, PA attorney. This attorney had offered me information, which turned out to be false, about a particular case before the court. I had included it in the pre-sentence report I had prepared.  At the sentencing hearing, the falsity of the information came to light and the judge faulted me for the error.  However, the U.S. Marshal spoke up for me privately with the judge who withdrew any sanction he would have entered against me.  Several weeks after this incident, I was walking past the office of this particular attorney and I saw him at the window beckoning me to come in.  I put my hand on my hip as if drawing my handgun and pointing my forefinger as if shooting him.  I did not go into his office and I never saw him again.  Weeks later, an article appeared in the daily newspapers that this attorney was found to be involved in questionable activities, mainly mishandling seniors' retirement funds, and he was ultimately disbarred from practicing law.

Another stressful incident occurred when an Assistant U.S. Attorney read to me from the prosecutor's file, the arrest record of a codefendant, rather than that of the defendant in whom I was interested.  At sentencing, the misinformation was corrected and in chambers, the judge asked where I had obtained the criminal record information. I revealed it was read to me by the Assistant U.S. attorney. Thereafter, the U.S. Attorneys' files were made available for any U.S. Probation Officer's personal review.

I remember when I was about 15 years of age, seeing a shiny, canary yellow Cadillac convertible touring in my South Philadelphia neighborhood, driven by a well dressed fellow who seemed to be known by everyone.  My impression was that he was a number writer, one who took bets on sporting events or just on the daily number.  He was known for his kindnesses to the needy families in the area and everybody liked "Jimmy" for his generosity and charitable efforts; he was especially liked by the ladies.

About 29 years later, while employed as a Federal Probation/Parole Officer I became aware of Jimmy's arrest on serious drug charges.   It was learned that a certain property in the vicinity of my family home had been under surveillance for some time as a drug den and when it was eventually raided resulted in the arrest of Jimmy and several others.

Convicted and sentenced to 15 years in prison, Jimmy was vilified by the judge who showed no mercy to drug offenders.   I recall being in the courtroom at sentencing when the judge rebuked Jimmy with an extensive, angry harangue causing Jimmy to blurt out, "What do you want from me?"   He was then returned to custody of the U.S. Marshal and subsequently transported to the penitentiary at Leavenworth, Kansas.

Several years later, he was paroled and I was visiting the neighborhood shoemaker, Domenic Sasso, a respected member of the community who repaired our family's shoes over the years.  He asked if I had the power to help Jimmy in some way, describing him as a broken man.  I told him the power was in the judge's hands and all that Jimmy could do was just abide by the rules of his release.  I understand that Jimmy was spending most of his time oil painting, a hobby he developed while in prison.

A couple of cases assigned to me for probation supervision happened to be residents of South Philadelphia, the area where I was reared, and both were former high school classmates of mine.   At the initial interview, I stressed my position to them, reviewed the rules that were in place, and that despite our earlier friendship, any violation of these rules would bring about some undesired action. Both cases expired without incident, but I remember that one of these two individuals had shown evidence in the earlier years of our friendship, when several of us played cards together, that he would likely be in trouble with the law at some future date.   Several years later, I learned through one of his relatives that he had become heavily involved in gambling and had in fact gambled away his mother's entire savings. What brought him to the Federal court's attention was his fraudulent approval of mortgage applications and accepting bribes.

One of the individuals that I supervised in the upscale area of Montgomery County was an importer/exporter, Sylvan Schulman, who violated Federal law by importing a supply of Tussah Silk from Red China. He had no prior record of arrest and he bore a good reputation in the community and business circles. He was sentenced to a one year probation term and a $500.00 fine. He paid the fine and his probation expired routinely. Interesting is the fact that he lived in this upscale area occupied chiefly by those in the higher income bracket, and in order to appear on equal status with his neighbors, he said, although he had no air conditioning in his late model Lincoln sedan, he rode with the windows closed while he was in his home area, no matter how humid it was, just to allow his neighbors to think his car was air conditioned.

Many cases were not straightforward. Edna Powers was a practical nurse, who was the caretaker of an 82-year-old widower who owned an upscale residence in Montgomery County. He was a paraplegic and needed constant attention. He could only move his wheelchair short distances, and one morning he was found dead at the bottom of the stairway. Edna was suspected of causing his fall because of her prior history. She had lost her husband several years earlier when he accidentally fell down a stairwell and broke his neck. After an investigation of her involvement in her client's death it was declared to be accidental. However, serious questions remained because a Will, executed two years earlier and determined to be completely legal, bequeathed her client's entire estate to

Edna.  She was on Federal probation at the time, serving a 5 year term for Medicare fraud. She had a prior record of arrest that allowed suspicion to hover over her, not only because of her husband's death, but because of an earlier charge of false impersonation as the mother of the Gerber babies (Gerber Baby Food Fame).  That charge resulted in a short term of probation and a heavy fine imposed in the local court.

There are neighborhood resources that exist of people who are of valuable assistance to law enforcement.  I met Alice Thorne who operated a "7 - Eleven" store in a seedy section of Chester.  She was recommended to me by one of the city's police officers as a reliable source of information of the community and its members.  I benefited from information she gave me on numerous occasions.

Alice was a brassy, outspoken blonde whose language matched that of the many customers with whom she dealt. One afternoon, while I was visiting at her store, two well-dressed black males entered, one of whom I recognized as a former probationer of mine, also a resident of the general area.  I was on the far side of the store when they entered and was hidden from view by various displays.  This man identified himself as a detective with the local police force.  I don't know if he saw me or not, I was in my usual attire, suit, white shirt, tie and felt hat, but there was one other person in the store at the time.  I could only surmise that even if he saw me, but didn't recognize me, he certainly saw another person was also present.  He purchased a pack of gum and the two men left.  I mentioned to Alice that it seemed obvious that our presence may well have prevented a robbery.  On the other hand it was possible, but unlikely, that he just wanted a pack of gum.  However, I would point out that Alice, a savvy street smart woman and a handgun expert, was probably ready for action which fortunately did not occur.

I must comment about one of the Federal judges who always seemed to go a bit farther than was necessary with follow up action on cases he sentenced. One involved a former police officer dismissed from the force for drunkenness as well as his violation of federal law. The judge had sentenced Gene Baker to 3 years probation for postal theft.

Gene was a very mild, gentlemanly type person and every time I visited him at home, his wife berated him almost constantly not allowing him to forget that he lost a lifetime job. His resulting home life was clearly a miserable one and the taunting attitude that prevailed each time I visited, revealed to me that his escape from her verbal barrage encouraged his alcoholism. I convinced him to attend AA meetings but even that didn't sway her verbal battering. She didn't appear to offer him one iota of support. I wondered if she had a direct line to the judge as he would call me almost weekly directing me to meet with them evenings to offer them counseling. I couldn't tell the judge that the wife did not appear to be a candidate for counseling, and while I did visit as directed, I doubted the wife's attitude would change. It was apparent that this judge failed to realize that the wife needed attention from a professional marriage counselor if she wanted the marriage to last, or an attorney to proceed with a divorce, for she showed no interest in offering some sorely needed support. Surprisingly, Gene's probation term expired without further incident.

Another case sentenced by this particular judge, was that of Harry Doubet, a 60-year-old realtor, married with grown children and no prior arrest record. His offense was improperly approving a mortgage application, for which he served a two year probation term. He completed his probation satisfactorily with no indication that the court would ever hear from him again. Yet despite the fact that his sentence had expired, the judge directed me to keep in touch with Mr. Doubet and submit a report to him every three months. Mr. Doubet was perplexed by the judge's order but he chose not to voice any objection and that he would accept our occasional visit as social.

One more of this judge's sentencings was that of Jack Dittman. I inherited this case when he moved into my district and a warrant was extant for his violating his probation by leaving the State without the court's permission. One summer day, while touring my district, I saw Jack, a gambler, who was known to most of the officers in our office, sitting outside one of the store fronts on South Street, a business section of South Philadelphia. I approached him, identified myself and informed him of the warrant charging him with violating his probation. He said he knew he'd eventually be picked up and he readily accompanied me to the U.S. Marshal's office. At a subsequent violation hearing before the judge, he asked me if I told Mr. Dittman why he was in violation of his probation, and I responded that he knew full well why he was here. The judge repeated his question asking, "But did you tell him he was in violation because he was out of the State without permission?" and I answered "No, your honor." With that he dismissed the violation charge and Mr. Dittman was free to return to the community, despite the fact that he did violate the special condition that this judge had imposed, a paradoxical action.

Yet another interesting case was that of Joseph Coach, a Navy Seal serving during WWII, who was considered one of several war heroes, medaled for having been involved in a number of dangerous missions including the Tokyo bay maneuver.  He was described as an expert in elevator repair and he was employed by the Otis firm both before and after his military service.  Somehow, he became involved in robbing banks with witnesses describing how fleet he was vaulting over counters and moving with daring speed.  Eventually he was apprehended and sentenced to a long prison term; his attorney entered an appeal to reduce his prison sentence.  I was assigned to do a follow up investigation on Mr. Coach and I met his wife, a demure shy and attractive person who was overwhelmed by her husband's involvement in bank robberies.  Mr. Coach had a picture of his attorney's daughter on the wall of his cell, according to another attorney, rather than that of his attractive wife.  It appeared to me and others in the office that the excitement of his four years as a Navy Seal during the war years had an effect on Mr. Coach who returned home to a quiet, non-adventurous life, lacking the excitement and challenges he had faced in the service, hence the robberies.  But why his wife's picture did not adorn his cell wall was a mystery.

Richard Bard, a 28-year-old, well built, very neat dresser, who could easily pass as an Ivy League college student, was on probation for forging U.S. Treasury checks. Married with a wife who was pregnant with their first child, Richard worked irregularly as a caddy at a local golf course. His wife came to my office one day to report that he was seeing another woman and she knew this because a $500.00 check written by him was returned to her for insufficient funds.  She said there had been other checks returned as well which she made good from her earnings as a secretary.  She had questioned Richard about it and he admitted he had a relationship with another woman for several weeks and that he had purchased an "engagement ring" for her.

In a subsequent interview, I informed him that the bad checks represented a violation of his probation. I later discussed this matter with the sentencing judge, making him aware of the brazen infidelity as well as the several bad checks, and he ordered Mr. Bard to appear before him to answer the violation charges. Richard remained mute at the hearing and the judge revoked his probation and sentenced him to a term of two years imprisonment. His wife had been advised about the hearing but declined to appear and said she had no further interest in him and planned to be a single mother.

Richard, committed to the Federal penitentiary at Lewisburg, Pa., subsequently appealed his violation sentence, causing me to appear at a hearing in the U.S. District Court in the Middle District of Pennsylvania, as he claimed I fabricated the charges against him. However, the judge upon hearing all the facts dismissed the case and Richard served the full two years of his sentence. It was evident that he knew he had no case but felt he'd inconvenience me by accusing me, causing me to travel and be away from home and family. He was that kind of guy.

When I started working at the Federal probation/parole office, I was assigned to cover certain postal zones in the South Philadelphia area as well as the county of Montgomery. The officer assigned to the Delaware County area, lived in Lehigh County which was many miles from his assigned district. He asked me to trade counties with him as his wife was seriously ill and he wanted to be closer to home to administer to her needs more conveniently. This change was approved by the Chief Probation Officer, and I too benefited from the change because I lived in Delaware County and also could be back at home if needed within minutes notice. My workweek was actually a 24/7 day schedule that usually exceeded the 40 hour week.  An example of how my work schedule could be changed at a moment's notice happened one summer while I was on vacation and on the beach in Sea Isle City, NJ.  My son came to the beach to tell me of a telephone call from the office in Philadelphia, which required that I cut my vacation short and report to the office.  This was part of the job.  This particular need prevailed because a member of my caseload had been arrested and I had information not yet in the record, but of importance to the authorities.

One of the cases in my assigned district involved a woman whom I will call Margie, about 30 years of age, who along with her husband was charged in a major illegal drug operation, the importation and distribution of heroin.  She happened to be a daughter of a family living in my home neighborhood.  This family consisted of six daughters ranging in age from 10 to 27 years of age, and one son in his late 20s.  The son was a retarded but friendly fellow and was frequently away from home, just traveling the road.  During the course of my pre-sentence investigation, I learned that the 27-year-old was married to a friend of mine with whom I had worked at the Westinghouse Turbine Division several years earlier.  After discussing this case with him, I learned that his father-in-law had violated each of his daughters when  they reached puberty, that my friend's wife, prior to their marriage revealed to him that she was a victim of the father and that she had severed all relationships with her parents.  Regrettably, her mother was fully aware of the sexual violations but never did anything about it.

Margie admitted that the information about her father was correct and that she was one of his victims.  Prior to sentence, the judge asked that I identify the father who planned to be in court at sentencing, saying, "I want to get a look at that SOB."  The judge appeared in his robe at the door below the Bench, where the U.S. Marshal normally appeared, nodding in disbelief as I pointed to the father who was seated directly in front of me.  Margie was sentenced to 15 years in prison and her husband was sentenced at a later hearing to 20 years.

Another case that drew the attention of the South Philadelphia community was that of Frank Simone, who played a minor role in an illegal still operation and was placed on a short term of probation.  Frank had dropped out of school at 16, he never had a steady job and wrote numbers for a while and was known for receiving and selling stolen goods.  While on probation he became involved with a group of organized crime figures, and word was out that he was a "snitch", an informer who was not to be trusted.  An FBI investigation had been in process for some time and when a few arrests were made of members of this particular group, Frank was an immediate suspect of disloyalty.  His body was found in a burlap bag behind a Food Fair market in South Philadelphia, with bullet wounds to the head.

A notable case under my supervision was that of William C. Colepaugh, a traitor of the WWII era.  A military tribunal convicted him of treason in 1945 and he was sentenced to death by hanging.  The details of this case were most interesting and while his trial was closed to the press and the public, details did emerge and were published nationally; some elaboration is here included.

Colepaugh, a resident of Connecticut, was not a very good student in school, failing in several courses and so his mother, who inherited substantial monies upon the demise of her husband, a successful plumber, enrolled him in a military prep school, the Admiral Farragut Academy, in New Jersey.  After graduation, he enrolled in the Massachusetts Institute of Technology as an engineering student, but failed to meet minimum standards and was flunked out.  He displayed anti-social tendencies early in life and his behavior grew progressively worse over the years. He joined the U.S. Naval Reserve in 1943, but after only 3 months, was discharged due to disciplinary problems and "for the good of the service."

Infatuated with Germany, he began associating with German sailors and attended German events including a birthday celebration for Adolph Hitler at the German Consulate. He soon displayed an interest in going to Germany and joined the Merchant Marines sailing on a ship that stopped in Lisbon, Portugal. There he jumped ship and found his way to Germany where he tried to join the army, but instead, because of his anti-American attitude, he was enrolled in a spy training center operated by Germany's SS. After training in sabotage, explosives, and methods of secreting information, he was partnered with one, Erich Gimple, a German-born radio expert who had extensive spy training.

Gimple wasn't keen on Colepaugh who could not speak German, but he accepted him as a partner because of his expressed hatred of America. They were transported in a U-boat on a two month journey across the Atlantic and remained on the ocean floor off the coast of Maine for several days to avoid detection. When it was determined that conditions were safe the submarine surfaced and the pair boarded a rubber raft and rowed to shore on November 29, 1944. The raft was tethered to a line from the submarine so that when they reached shore, the raft could be towed back to the U boat and not found as evidence of infiltrators. But the tether broke and two crewmen had to swim from the submarine to recover the raft and tow it back to their vessel. Colepaugh and Gimple were now on their own to infiltrate industry and accomplish assigned goals, sending information back to Germany by a radio they were to build.

They arrived on shore dressed in expensive topcoats and fedoras, clothing that was untypical of Americans, especially in the wooded Maine area where they had disembarked.  They carried two suitcases, one of which contained spy gear and the $60,000.00 in U.S. currency they had been given to finance their mission; the other contained items of clothing.  On the night they came ashore, they were seen, walking on the snow- covered road, by a resident driving home from a card game, and she felt they looked so strange in their clothing carrying the two suitcases that she reported what she had seen to the sheriff the next morning, but by this time they were already in New York.

Gimple and Colepaugh were not getting along too well and it was learned, after their arrest, that Colepaugh was spending the money freely, enjoying the high life and forgetting that they had a specific mission.  Soon, Colepaugh developed a fear of Gimple, so he took the suitcase with the cash, now about $50,000.00,  and the spy gear, and checked into an upscale midtown hotel.  He looked up an old school chum and enjoyed their reunion for a few days.  On December 26, 1944, after discussing his situation with his friend, he decided to turn himself in to the FBI.  On information provided by Colepaugh, Gimple was arrested four days later.

They were brought to trial for espionage before a military tribunal, and after only an hour and a half of testimony, they were sentenced to death by hanging.  Their executions were scheduled for April 15, 1945, but President Franklin d. Roosevelt' death on April 12, 1945, caused their executions to be postponed for a month.  However, the war had ended with Germany's surrender and President Harry S. Truman commuted their sentences to life in prison.  Records indicate that because of Colepaugh's cooperation, his sentence was further commuted to 30 years. The cooperation was considered because of his voluntary surrender and his assistance in capturing his codefendant within days.

After serving 12 years in the maximum security prison at Leavenworth, Kansas, he was transferred in 1957, because of his good adjustment, to the minimum security prison at Lewisburg, PA. Records of his transfer revealed that his property that was shipped with him consisted of dozens of books on philosophy, architectural drawing and numerous technical manuals he studied preparing for his future.

He was paroled in 1962, and on his initial visit to the parole office, he disclosed that he had purchased an automobile as he was living in the adjacent county and needed transportation. The vehicle was parked on the main city street, just outside the Federal building, and looking out the window of my office I saw the vehicle was a fire red 1961 Pontiac convertible.

The trade he learned while confined allowed him to obtain work initially as a draftsman and metal fabricator but soon he secured work in a steel fabricating shop that built desks, lockers and other metal office products. He earned $35.00 monthly while imprisoned, but he was now earning $660.00 monthly, at the Penn Oaks Company. He did so well that when the owner wanted to retire he sold the business to Mr. Colepaugh. He adjusted very well under supervision and was released from parole by reason of expiration of sentence.

Another interesting case was that of James Conley, a 63-year- old who was serving a 25 year sentence for bank robbery. He was an inmate at the Federal penitentiary in Leavenworth, Kansas, where he had served 10 years, and because of his good behavior he was then transferred to the minimum security prison at Lewisburg, Pennsylvania. His job while confined was working as a gardener where he excelled tending to all the gardens surrounding the prison's grounds. His adjustment was so satisfactory that he earned the title of "trustee" which allowed him special privileges not accorded the usual inmate. He was allowed to move almost freely outside the prison walls without the need to seek prior permission.

After serving a little over 15 years, he presented himself as a worthy candidate for parole, and the Parole committee granted his parole. James looked much older than his 63 years when he reported to me for his initial interview. Considering his criminal history and the many years of incarceration in several different prisons, time had certainly taken its toll.

Despite his early behavior history along with his criminal background, he appeared to be a rather meek, gentleman type of person, rather than the rugged, brash individual that I expected to meet. We discussed the rules of his release and he stressed he had no intention of violating the trust placed in him, that all of his antisocial behavior was behind him.

Just three weeks later, when J. was living in a small apartment, he came to my office requesting that he be returned to the institution as he didn't think he could make it outside prison walls. He said he felt totally lost in this free atmosphere and was most uncomfortable with all the changes that had taken place since his confinement so many years ago.

James pleaded to be sent back to prison where he had a strong sense of security, a job he enjoyed and responsibilities he was capable of handling. Here was a truly sad situation, an offender who had paid for his mistakes, but his frequent and long imprisonments had completely institutionalized him. (This is the situation that Al Sailer describes in his paper in Appendix 1). While imprisoned James had no decisions to make; he was told when to arise, when to retire, when and what to eat. All of this was done on a regular schedule and he had no worries whatsoever.

After considerable correspon-dence with the U.S. Bureau of Prisons, a special action was taken and he was eventually transported back to the penitentiary where he was soon assigned to his old job as prison gardener. It is almost bizarre to hear of a case of a paroled inmate accepted back without having violated the conditions of his release. It may be safely assumed that this individual was so disturbed by his release to a world so different from the world he knew, that he surely would have resorted to some crime to get back to the "home" and security he enjoyed in confinement.

There's an area in the city of Chester, Pa. called the Fairgrounds. Although it sounds like the name of a carnival or playground this is a misnomer as it was not a fun place. In the 1970s, Chester had the highest crime rate in the country and this was my district. Rapes, robberies and even murders were commonplace here.

When visiting in one of the high rise dwellings, it was wise to climb the stairs with your back to the wall so that you had a view of both directions while ascending or descending. I usually planned to be in this particular area during the early morning hours while most tenants were still sleeping. On this particular morning I was about to enter one of the houses in this project development when a police officer patrolling the area, asked what I was doing in this area. I was dressed in my usual attire, suit, white shirt, tie and felt hat. I flashed my ID, showing that I was a Federal officer and said I was checking on a member of my caseload. He immediately responded, "You better get the hell out of here as something is alleged to be going down today." I took his suggestion and left. I could return another time, even though no day is any safer than any other in this particular city.

Of all my cases, Alfred Sailer, is the most memorable. He was the son of a former newspaper editor who had a very strong, domineering personality, and according to Al, she exerted extreme control over her children. Alfred had two sisters; one was unmarried and had a doctorate in education with a very responsible position in the local school system. The other was a housewife in an unhappy marriage and also under the stressful control of her domineering mother. During the course of my association with Alfred, this sister committed suicide by stepping into the path of a moving vehicle. She left a note describing her plan to kill herself and Al blamed his mother's excessive controlling as making her feel suicide was her only means of escape.

Sailer's failing began when he went AWOL from the U.S. Air Force and found it easy to exist by writing false checks. He was on probation for check writing and had been committed to Federal prison for violating his probation sentence. I became acquainted with him when he was released on parole. He was to live with his mother whose residence was in the area assigned to me. He was under my supervision for only a brief period before he broke into another auto and stole a check book which he used to his advantage. This was his typical modus operandi. At this point in his life, when I met him, he had served at least 20 years in various prisons for similar thefts, as well as forgeries; and the interstate aspect of his dalliances brought him to the attention of Federal authorities.

At his probation violation hearing, it was my duty as his supervising probation officer, to review the circumstances of his violation, and on the basis of my report the county revoked his probation and imposed the 5 year prison term that had originally been suspended.  He was then remanded to the Federal Penitentiary at Lewisburg, Pa.

About three months later, in December 1971, Al sent a hand-drawn Christmas greeting card to me.  This was a unique piece of work, showing the outline of the face of Santa Claus on the outside of the card, with the face cutout to allow his self-portrait on the inner page to peer through.

The message contained several self-deprecating lines that Al had printed on the inside, indicating that he wanted to assume that he held himself responsible for his return to prison, and that he alone is responsible for the time he must now serve.

Upon seeing the detail of the drawing on that card I sent him a letter complimenting him on his artistic ability and originality.  Thus began a long and valuable correspondence, offering rewarding information to one another, and our observations on various issues of life.

He sent a letter in response and wrote:

"When I entered my cell last night after returning from work, and saw the letter marked U.S. District Court, I thought 'more bad news,' but when I opened it and found it was your reply to my letter and card, I was overwhelmed with relief.  Actually, I had given up hearing from you and please know that I appreciate your response.

"Perhaps it was just coincidence that I received your letter on the same day I went before the parole board.  This was supposedly my parole hearing on the sentence I am now serving.  I had prepared a brief statement that was well grounded; however, it was not the kind of statement these people want to hear. And my attitude wasn't that you'd expect it to be, all things considered.  I cannot pretend to be in awe of these people with their power over me.  While it is enormous, I cannot be intimidated with them anymore.  As a consequence, I am rather obnoxious to them since I fail to be impressed.  The trouble with these hearings is that you are really not permitted to voice your own view; they give it their own spin to support a decision they've already made before you even enter the room.  I had only read a couple of lines of my statement when they interrupted me and terminated the interview.  My statement wasn't very long, and with it they could have made an intelligent and valid decision.  Without it they handed me another injustice which serves merely to justify the persecution I already feel."

He added, "The future doesn't hold much for me as there are four detainers against me for bad checks. The Interstate Compact says detainers must be disposed on within 180 days, but here it is almost 18 months and they're still against me. What can I say; the wheels of justice seem to ignore their real purpose."

During his incarceration on this particular sentence, he drew several pieces with the pen and ink medium and sent them to his mother's home suggesting that I visit there to comment on them.  I did so and reviewed five different pieces he created. In my opinion these were truly artistic drawings that should be evaluated by authorities in the art field.

With Al's permission, I made an appointment with a member of the Pennsylvania Academy of Fine Art and took these 5 drawings there for review.  Several days later, I received a call that they were available for my pick-up.  They had been determined to be true works of art, but it was recommended that the artist should resist the maudlin and get into other more acceptable subjects.  It was also suggested I speak with the owner of the Walnuts Gallery in Philadelphia for possible display and perhaps even sale of this art work.  A visit to the gallery produced quite favorable comments; it was felt that Al did excellent work but that the subject of all his samples was a bit too strong and on just one theme. Copies of his drawings are shown in Appendix 2.

Eventually, I wrote to Al reporting on the comments of these art reviewers and he was elated, actually exhilarated, and extremely pleased by their comments. These favorable reports caused Al to become more dedicated in his efforts and allowed him to produce some very interesting pieces.

In my correspondence with him, I mentioned various happenings occurring in my life, personal as they were, letting him see that we all experience stress in our daily activities but we find suitable responses in dealing with them.  The solutions do no occur overnight, but we persist and do not go over the deep end in attempting to resolve them.  At first, I didn't keep his letters, but I soon realized they carried some important revelations showing the introspective developments that were occurring in Al's attitude and his thinking process.  They displayed the changes that were developing, allowing him to see that his responses to problems were improper and could have been handled in a more acceptable manner.

I include some excerpts from many of the letters that passed between Al and me that offered some introspective comments of interest.

His letters were sometimes several pages long but I found them always interesting.  After some months, he wrote:

"Sometimes when I'm writing one of my lengthy diatribes to you, I think to myself, why am I loading this guy with my meanderings when he surely has more important things to do?  But then I think further and realize it's because you're the only one I feel comfortable with in revealing my inner thoughts and recognizing that you are truly interested and listening. Everybody needs somebody who is willing to listen."

"When I return to my cell after my day's work, finding a response from you puts a spark in my life and lifts my spirits. Being able to correspond with you, knowing there is a link that does not exist when writing to a parent or a relative, where you can unload and feel some relief from the pressures and anxieties that build up in these places is a real value to me."

I asked Al in one of my early letters, "Considering the many times you've been confined over the years how do you tolerate being away from home and family?" And he wrote, "It's very difficult, but the only way you can do it is to put everything and everyone out of your life and mind. It's the most difficult thing to accept and accomplish but it's something you must do not only for yourself and your own peace of mind, but for those related to you. You learn to see this world as reality and the outside world as something far removed from you. You have absolutely no control over things out there and you're helpless to do anything about them."

In another letter, he asked me, "Would you answer a question for me, please? I'm wondering, if after reading all that material I wrote and what I've said in my many letters, has your own attitude regarding people like me changed? I'm thinking of a more liberal, concerned type of judgment for the recidivist which I am."

I answered, "Al, you've certainly caused me to wonder about you with all the time you've spent in custody status. You've got a distorted view of the consequences of your actions, obviously: you keep getting caught up in your check writing sprees, failing to recognize the risk of your actions and that you will get caught and ultimately penalized. It's like 'Ground Hog Day,' a re-run activity.

Your failure to see this would properly place you in the category of psychopathic behavior, but with getting to know you through the caliber of your writings and the years you've wasted, I cannot figure what clouds your thinking."

I am saddened when I think what Al may have contributed with the manuscript he wrote during his years in custody, which could be a valued contribution if viewed by those in the penology field.  Al had said he wanted me to have the manuscript and it seems appropriate, as he is now deceased, to include it along with his case history.  His thoughts on "a view from the bottom," are provoking and worthy of consideration.

To pass on a little humor, I put a paragraph in one of my letters to Al that "riding home from the office in a torrential rain storm the past week, the roads were so flooded that I had to drive so far out of my way that the normal half hour ride took two hours to reach home. I jumped out of the car, locked the car door and ran to my back door.  I didn't know why I ran as I was already soaked to the skin, and only then did I realize I had left my keys in the ignition.  So there I was, locked out of my car and my home in the rain feeling stupid.  What I needed was a hanger or a piece of wire, so I looked around and saw my wife's bucket and the handle would fit my need.  I kept pounding that bucket against the wall until I dislodged the handle and met with success in unlocking the car door and retrieving my keys.  I had to laugh about it later."

In Al's next letter he wrote, "You talk about locking yourself out of the car in the pouring rain, I did that once when I was on the check route. I went into a place, cashed a check and was trying to make a quick departure when I discovered no keys.  I went to my car at curbside and saw they were still in the ignition so I walked about 4 blocks away, and sat in a bar until everything closed for the day.

Borrowed a coat hanger and did the same thing you did. But I was wet from sweat when I finally got the door open, not from the rain as you were."

One of Al's letters mentioned that just being jailed while awaiting sentence could be described as adequate punishment in some instances, and I recalled a case where that was a fact. I cited a case where I had completed a pre-sentence report several years ago on a bank teller who embezzled $135,000.00. He bought a new auto, a boat, and dined his family royally. This was his first offense; he came from a good family background and had every attribute that showed him to be a good candidate for probation. The judge had committed him to a three year prison term, and days after he was sentenced, I visited him at the Detention Center to conduct a pre-commitment interview.

This involved telling him what he could expect in the institution and answering any questions he may have had. Well, I got to the second tier of the prison where the 4' x 4' interviewing booths were located and this fellow just sat there crying silently. He didn't need to speak, indeed he failed to utter one spoken word; yet, I heard every word he wanted to say. This fellow was a great big guy, over 6' tall, a little obese, maybe 220 pounds, not the type you'd expect to see cry. He was one of those individuals who just needed that one day in custody, and it was enough punishment. We would never hear from him again.

Fortunately, the judge must have had second thoughts about this guy as he called me a few days later and asked me what I thought. I told him what the interview was like at the Detention Center and a couple of days later he amended the sentence to five years probation with the condition he make restitution. He made the restitution, resumed a good family life and he adjusted quiet well with the case closing by reason of termination of sentence. He ended up as a truck driver earning a very good income.  I heard from him the next Christmas holiday when he sent me a greeting card with a photo of his expanding family. He would likely never be before the court again, and it exemplified that "one day was enough."

In one of my letters, I commented on the recent murders of the Warden and Associate Warden at the Philadelphia Detention Center by two inmates, with reference to capital punishment.  Al responded briefly that a forked tongue is present here since I may be advocating killing on the one hand, but sanctioning it on the other. His observation was that these two killers should have been housed in a maximum security institution.  And he was probably right.

Elaborating further on the subject of punishment in another of his letters, he wrote, "Punishment to me reeks of vengeance. The contention is that while the criminal is capable of responsible behavior, his rationale is inconsistent and fluctuates with the tide of his immature and unstable emotions."  He added, "We aren't children you're trying to 'potty train', and we are not children but adults, retarded adults perhaps, but adults just the same. Actually, we are immature, our minds haven't developed nor have our emotions.  We are still very much like children, but we do not have their innocence.  We are suspicious and distrustful and tend to twist the most innocent situation into something that is ugly.  You might just say we are paranoid. If you say to one of us you're wrong, this is how it is, this is how to do it, you'd be wasting your time and doing us harm, because you'd be prodding our obstinacy and therefore bolstering our suspicion of you."

In regard to prison treatment, he didn't say we should close the prisons but does say we should change their image.  He explained, "I came in at the tail end of the reform method and I went through the correction method and the rehabilitation jumbo.  Now we're getting a new method, it has no name yet.  The guards wear sports blazers with an embroidered 'C' on the jacket pocket and bright yellow or pretty blue shirts and lovely gold ties.  Now they're called 'Correction Officers'.  Joe, for Christ's sake, these are the same guys who used to be called turnkeys, guards and custodial officers.  What we need is real change where the purpose is to habilitate.  Forget about education, forget about a skill, forget about proper work habits.  Give us proper 'thinking' habits and the rest will fall in place."

During his time serving terms in various prisons, both local and Federal, Al compiled a rather impressive manuscript of the institution's programs, general conditions with an alpha omega view, by an "inside man" of the justice system as a whole, and he titled this manuscript "A View From The, Bottom".  Because it presents the criminal justice system as seen by an inmate it is an apt title. It is included as Appendix 1.

While confined, Al took part in studies of dentistry, and in fact aided fellow prisoners who had minor dental problems, such as adjusting and repairing dentures. Although he was trained to make dentures and partial plates and bridges, he related he was called upon more frequently to re-set broken jaws.  However, he became quite adept at this denture making business and being artistically inclined, he even textured the gum portions making the dentures more realistic.

With this gained ability, after his release, he made a full set of dentures for his mother. To assist him in his quest for employment, I spent hours daily driving him to job opportunities, mostly to dental practitioners.  He described his experiences of success of making dental plates but the fact that his history of their production was in a penal institution, and not in an accredited training facility, failed to create any real interest in his being hired.

With Al's permission, I discussed his case with a reporter at the local newspaper who had been a classmate of mine at college, who felt an article on Al's background and release appeared to be a most interesting item and could be of some value to him. The write-up in the Delaware County Daily Times resulted in Al being commissioned to do a drawing for a resident in a nearby community for which he was paid $200.00 and this renewed his self confidence in becoming productive in some legitimate endeavors. However, his subjects were still on the dark side. This particular commission was made for a white woman who was having a hidden love affair with a black man who was then serving time in a local jail. Al's rendition showed the lovers in a garden with a large apple in the foreground and with a snake coiling around the two figures. I had driven Al to the buyer's home to make the delivery and he was very apprehensive fearing she would not like his interpretation. When he emerged from the residence, however, he was overjoyed that she was most happy with his rendition of her affair.

It became evident to me that Al was going to succeed in making his return to the free community work this time, and as his supervising parole officer it was my duty to assist him in this regard. He lived only a couple of miles from my home and I felt it would good to let him into my life to see how we enjoyed our lives, that he had it in his power to lead a lawful productive life without resorting to his past endeavors.

His parole term expired without further incident and he subsequently developed a relationship with a woman his age. Previously, in his early background he had several girlfriends, usually younger than he, and one was a former

Miss America contestant.  The woman he was now courting seemed to be a good stabilizing influence on his, and she had relatives in New England where they eventually settled. Al secured work in a hardware store, did quite well in the operation of the business, and when the owner wanted to retire, a deal was arranged whereby Al became the new owner.

We continued to correspond fairly regularly and his mother and sister also kept me informed as to how well things were going for Al.  He appeared to have made a new life, happy with work and love. Just when things were going so well he fell on an icy walkway and fractured his spine. Not long afterward I learned that he died from complications and was buried in his hometown in New England.  His sister and mother expressed appreciation to me saying they felt I was responsible for turning Al's life around.  But I think it was Al's doing, he turned his own life around, acquiring a new, and more realistic sense of values and goals.  As his supervising patrol officer, I was there as a listener, allowing him to reflect his concerns and to help guide him to proper goals, offering him guidance and counsel on a regular basis. Corresponding with him and bringing him into my family home may have been influential in realigning his sense of values.

Through our correspondence, while he was serving his sentence, he knew I was a member of one of the Philadelphia Mummers' String Bands.  After his release he designed a 3 x 4 foot poster exhibiting a multi-faced bust showing a helmeted male, holding a wrench/banjo and a significant theme showing that the string band members had varied occupations. This was so impressive that the band developed it into a three-dimensional project and it now hangs in the Philadelphia Mummers' Museum.  Al would certainly have been proud to know that a piece of his art was found worthy enough to adorn the wall of one of Philadelphia's premier Art Institutions.

In many of those cases where the offender has successfully completed his/her sentence without resorting to any subsequent unlawful behavior, it provides a degree of psychic satisfaction
to the supervising probation/parole officer by allowing him/her to feel that the time and attention devoted to that case was not wasted.  It is generally in the parolee's own aptitude to do the right thing that allows successful termination of supervision to prevail. It becomes evident that if the parolee truly desires to make a good adjustment he/she will, with guidance or counsel being available if he seeks it.  There will always be a need for probation/parole officers just as the need for prisons will remain a necessary part of society.

In 1978, I had retired from the Federal justice system having exited early due to the fast approaching mandatory retirement age.  I had met the new owner of Schmidt's brewery a few years before when I was a Federal Probation/Parole office and had completed a pre-sentence investigation on him for mislabeling beer kegs to earn a better profit.  He was sentenced to a term of probation and I was his supervising probation officer.  His excellent adjustment under supervision was reported to the court and his sentence was terminated in 1976 one year earlier than the normal expiration date.

In 1977, knowing I faced mandatory retirement at the age of 55 years I decided to seek other employment before reaching that age, and I was aware of an opening soon to occur with the Pennsylvania Board of Parole Commission as the Board was to be increased from four to six members. Recognizing that I would benefit from political help, and knowing William Pflaumer, a businessman who was acquainted with a Pennsylvania Senator and a prominent western Pennsylvania judge, I visited him and advised him of my plan to retire, and of the job prospect I had in mind. He said he was aware of a possible job opening in the area and suggested I sit tight until I heard from him. A few days later, he called and offered me a job with his firm as an assistant to the Purchasing Director. Salary was discussed; I accepted and became a Schmidt's employee two weeks later.

It was January, 1978, when I started working at the brewery and it wasn't long before I became aware of certain deals being made by department heads with various vendors. This information came to light when a vendor called me to allow him to be a supplier for specific departments and he would give me a "free credit line" to Sears. Of course I declined, and suggested to Mr. Pflaumer that all purchasing should be done by the purchasing department and not by individual departments. He immediately agreed and within a month, three department heads turned in their resignations.

Mr. Pflaumer and the Treasurer had reviewed the preponderance of labels in stock for the different brands of beer that were over-ordered well beyond the need, and that resulted in the Purchasing Director's dismissal and my subsequent promotion to Director.

Looking back to the day I visited Mr. Pflaumer when I was seeking his help in getting some political support in my quest to be appointment to the State Parole Commission, I had no knowledge he was in the process of replacing his Purchasing Director, but I saw the impact of the phrase "being in the right place at the right time."

Now working as the Purchasing Director, I knew we had a need for some steel office equipment, and I saw that William Colepaugh's firm was listed as a potential supplier. I contacted him and with the quality, price, and availability being right, I gave him the business. At that time, I learned that he was happily married and had undergone surgery for removal of a brain tumor and it is my understanding that he died in 2005, from complications of Alzheimer's disease at 87 years of age.

The Christian Schmidt Brewing Company was headed for bankruptcy and Mr. Pflaumer recognized that as a major hauler for the company, his business was in jeopardy, so he decided to put in a bid for its purchase as he would not only save his trucking company but would see huge gains in his corporate profits. Pflaumer, a street smart individual, originally worked in his father's beer distributorship, but because the father was satisfied with his circumstances and had no interest in expanding the business, Billy decided to start his own distributorship. With one truck, $7,000.00, and an aggressive attitude to succeed, he bought up other distributorships, acquired many trucks and in time built an empire.

Due to a congenital eye defect, Mr. Pflaumer, known popularly as Billy, wore aviator style sunglasses to shade his pale blue pigmented eyes. His confident attitude and strong personality were displayed with the naming of his KMA Trucking Company, a pseudonym for "Kiss My Ass". Billy also owned a sprawling property at the New Jersey shore community known as "Beer World". On this 228 acre property, he had riding horses, a motorized trolley used to transport visitors wishing to tour the vast acreage, a large barn with various species of fowl and barn animals, and a motel of many rooms to house overnight guests. There was a large "fan boat", and a nine hole golf course, all to entertain visitors. In addition, he had a huge pavilion containing at least 50 picnic style tables and a restaurant style kitchen with a soda fountain. He used the property to entertain youth groups, various charitable organizations, as well as neighborhood communities and some business groups. Also on this property were a private swimming pool, a baseball field and three single homes used by immediate family members and other relatives.

In my social activities, I was involved with the Philadelphia String Bands Association, being President of The Original Trilby String Band, and one of my functions was to seek fee paying jobs which fees went toward the purchase of costumes for the annual New Year's Day celebration in Philadelphia. I was aware that the band had been hired by Schmidt's prior to Mr. Pflaumer's taking over the firm, so I took advantage of our earlier association and asked to perform for the brewery when the need for a band arose. Mr. Pflaumer said he had a job coming up and Trilby would be his band of choice, and he presented me with a $1,000.00 check as a deposit or payment in full depending on the length of the engagement. Well, I held onto that check for three weeks and not having received any word on a job for our band, I visited the brewery and returned the check to him and told him the band would be glad to accept payment when we actually did a job for his company.

The brewery was a successful venture and became the country's ninth largest brewery in 1980. With the largest beer distributorship and trucking company dominating the industry, Pflaumer's various enterprises grossed an estimate $215 million annually.

In 1981, Billy was found guilty of a new federal charge of evading $125,000.00 in excise taxes. He had been buying fuel oil from out of state to operate his Philadelphia brewery, and after appeals were exhausted, he was sentenced to three years imprisonment. The brewery at this time had been meeting difficulty with sales and couldn't compete with Budweiser. It wasn't long before a decision was made to sell, and the Schmidt brands were sold to Heilman Brewery in Wisconsin, and the Schmidt complex was sold in 1986 to a land developer. Billy had heart surgery in 1985 to replace a defective valve, and subsequently died of heart failure in 2002.

I have now been retired from the work force for almost 35 years, but I am still meeting interesting people. My associations are basically with the senior element rather than the criminal element of society.  These seniors are from all walks of life and all have very interesting stories to tell. But for me, looking back my career as a probation/parole officer tops them all.

Unfortunately, there still exist scheming members of society, who, while not violating the law, are present and ready to take advantage of others, especially senior citizens. In some circumstances these individuals may gravitate to more serious offenses and thus become the future cases of a probation or parole officer.  The circle of life will continue.

# APPENDIX 1

## A VIEW FROM THE BOTTOM
### By Al Sailer

The majority of people in our prisons today are persons who are confined as a result of aberrant behavioral patterns or guilty of defective judgments.  We see the criminal here as a professional whose primary concern is the successful commission of a crime.  "Successful commission of a crime" is to be defined in terms of escaping detection, apprehension, prosecution and punishment.  The professional criminal weighs every aspect of his act, prior to taking action and he will consider that the crime must meet at least three major requirements:  (1) sufficient personal gain, (2) ample opportunity of fulfillment and (3) minimum possibility of detection.  Next the possibility of being caught and punished must be considered.  Here the risk involved, coupled with the penalty for the crime must be weighed against the gain to be realized from the crime.

The professional criminal is a person who possesses an unusual amount of patience and self-discipline.  He must be astute, cunning, conniving and highly intelligent.  He must approach crime as a businessman and be financially capable of undertaking his venture.  But, like any other good businessman, he must be endowed with vision and foresight.  He should be prepared to meet any emergency, therefore, his starting capitol should adequately supply him with the equipment needed to do the job properly.  In addition, he must have competent legal representation and bail bonding fees in the event that the operation is a failure.

The most important prerequisites for the true criminal are:  stability, maturity and, of paramount importance, self-confidence.  However, this profile does not bear the slightest resemblance to the vast majority of the men and women who populate our prisons.  A large percentage are recidivists, and better than 35% are third and even fourth offenders.

Crimes against property dominate and in most instances the criminal realizes little, if any, monetary gain from the crime.  When he does, the penalty far exceeds any financial compensation he may have garnered from his efforts.

Very few crimes exhibit prior planning or intelligence, but show an extremely amateurish execution, making detection and apprehension appear to have been the ultimate goal of the criminal.  When arrested and taken into custody, these failures rarely possess cigarette or coffee money, much less, the price of a cheap attorney or bail monies.

Many, especially the recidivist, have no friends and their families have long since severed their relationship with them.  Upon contacting relatives and past acquaintances and reviewing the offender's past history, it is not surprising to learn that they had shown signs of anti-social behavior patterns for some time prior to making their "criminal debuts".  Their most distinguishing characteristics are immaturity and instability, which is evinced at the emotional, as well as the intellectual level.  Additionally, they are devoid of self-confidence.

The severest criticism and loudest repudiation of this analysis, will, astonishingly enough, come from those whom it depicts.  Such a reaction would tend to indicate that these people are incapable of making a realistic self-evaluation.  Or, it may be that they find it more palatable to accept themselves as failures, rather than have their mental infirmities exposed to account for their irrational behavior.

Actually neither is the case, for the criminal does not see himself as being mentally ill; nor does he see himself a failure.  Then just how does he rationalize his situation? What kind of reasoning and logic does he employ?

To answer these as well as the many questions which arise pertaining to his abnormal behavior patterns, the thinking apparatus of the entire group, with all of its complex machinations, must be studied and analyzed. Supposedly, this task was undertaken some time ago as we have specialists in this field who have assumed the professional titles of criminologists, penologists, psychiatrists, psychologists and sociologists, with having devised a successful formula for treating the malady.  While it is true they have invented some formidable sounding labels, such as "constitutional psychopaths" or "socio-psychopaths", this seems to have been the end rather than the beginning of their research.  Under the circumstances, it should not be considered unjust to contend that their study was incomplete or limited, or that their analysis was haphazard; or more simply, that perhaps it never progressed beyond the embryo stage.

By conventional standards, for an opinion to be acceptable, it must in any professional or scientific area, be expressed by highly qualified or eminently renowned technicians and supported with bonafide findings based on established precedents which remain consistent with proven theory.  However, in this particular area, there exists no valid criteria.  Those theories that have been put forth from time to time have developed some serious flaws.  After being subjected to extensive experimentation, it was discovered that while these theories may be applicable in isolated instances, they have little significant relationship to the problems evidenced by the group as a whole.

The thinking process which governs human behavior has been the object of much scientific investigation over the past Century. As a consequence, several theories have evolved. Two, or perhaps three, have emerged as being sufficiently sound enough to be considered as standard focal points of reference. A person exhibiting abnormal behavior patterns is examined, observed, and finally categorized in accordance with the particular theory espoused and practiced by the individual clinician responsible for the diagnosis. In most instances, any two clinicians who are asked to submit separate, independent opinions on the same subject, will disagree. Should their disagreement be exposed to public scrutiny, they will invariably settle their differences and each will hide behind the mysterious language barrier of their profession, later defining their earlier disagreement as pertaining to non-essential details and technicalities, they will be extremely voluble in declaring that basically they are in full accord in their overall evaluation of the individual's mental condition. They stoutly refuse to become actively involved in any matter relating to criminal prosecution. None dare to challenge the credibility of the McNaughton Rule for determining criminal responsibility.

Bigoted pedagogy has always handicapped progress. It is no less prevalent in the social-sciences than it is in any other field. The knowledgeable are intimidated by power and socio-political concepts and trends. Few have the determination or courage of a Galileo, willing to risk their security and position in pursuit of an unpopular cause, or to make an effort to rescue man from the fatal embrace if ignorance. Those who dare to challenge established philosophies and procedures must be prepared to have their own credentials challenged. The opinions and theories expressed herein were not conceived in an orthodox fashion, nor do they pretend to display raw and unsophisticated genius. Experience, combined with a wide variety of literature, will be the sole authority. What is found here are the discoveries made by a man who has spent a quarter of a century pondering his own dilemma in an effort to answer a question, which sooner or later confronts everyone in similar circumstances, namely, "WHAT AM I DOING HERE".

Government as well as society has given pragmatic sanction to a system of treating criminal offenders which system has proven itself quite unsound. The perpetuation of it would suggest ignorance, yet this is not the case, at least not entirely. While there is still much exploration to be done in the fields of penology and criminology, which necessarily will prove enlightening, the basic motivation for retarding change stems from the lamentable fact that the system has become an integral part of our country's economic machine.

The apprehension, prosecution and detention complex, along with their associate agencies in prevention and supervision, combined with the various administrative branches of the criminal justice system (Federal, State, County and Municipal), provide employment, either directly or indirectly, to almost a large portion of the work force on the country. Crime, and the constant threat of crime, can be credited with supporting or stimulating economic growth to some extent within almost every area of private enterprise and industry.

The mechanics of a successful economic system demands balance, harmony and stability. Supply cannot exceed demand. Therefore, in order for crime to be woven into the economic fabric of a nation, it must be synchronized with the fluctuating rhythm of its economic trends. But here the unpredictable element of human behavior requires that some mechanical apparatus be employed to govern the flow. This may appear to present an insoluble problem, if viewed from the standpoint of controlling the individual criminal's actions. However, once the problem is approached from the opposite direction, that is conviction and prison sentences for minor offenses at a time when the crime rate is at a low, will equal the same percentages for more serious crimes during a period when the crime rate is at a high. One other curious coincidence which cannot be overlooked is the more liberal use of suspended sentences, probations, paroles and pardons (which are not governed by any regulatory legislation, but are entrusted to the arbitrary whims of individual judges or parole and pardon authorities) during periods when more space is needed for warehousing. This is brought on by the more prevalent conditions of criminality as opposed to a much more discriminate utilization of these same remedies during a lull in criminal activity.

Human nature and the primitive instincts which still greatly influence men's thinking, provide a second, but none-the-less important reason for society's stubborn refusal to repudiate a barbaric criminal justice system that has proven itself, not only a failure, but an abominable contradiction to man's "professed Christian humanity". Even though crime and the present method of dealing with criminals has become an economic necessity, a new and much more humane method could be devised and gradually infiltrated into the economic pattern which would serve the same purpose. But it appears that the psychological makeup of society demands vengeance.

These primitive tendencies have long been recognized by those responsible for formulating public opinion on any controversial issue and have been instrumental in supplying them with the tools required to persuade and manipulate the thinking processes of the general public. Secret prejudices, latent degeneracy, ignorance, superstition and lack of intelligence have always been the stupid, but willing allies of hypocrisy and demagoguery. If man is to avoid being destroyed by his own weaknesses, he must first take cognizance of them by acknowledging them to himself. The same philosophy applies to any kind of a system, for if it has been conceived and implemented by man, it is therefore, as fallible as its creators and administrators.

Many quasi-logical arguments have been advanced to support the idea that punishment, and the criminal justice system as it exists today, is a necessary evil. Foremost among them is the contention that fear of punishment acts as a deterrent to crime. The logic underlying this presumably is that most individuals would resort to criminal behavior if it were possible to do so and escape retribution. Such a hypothesis denies the existence of two of man's most valued possessions, his honor and his integrity. To reason in this fashion is to charge mankind with unmitigated hypocrisy and places him on a contemporary level with the criminal.

About 1% of the population becomes so alienated from society that they develop a deep seated neurosis. As a means of dealing with their illness (at least the superficial symptoms), this group resorts to anti-social or criminal behavior. With some, it is an effort to gain a measure of recognition in the hopes of finding understanding and help. With others it is simply a final act of rebellion against a society that ignores and refuses to accept them.

The normal individual is guided by the conventional concept of maintaining status and finds his security in belonging. All but that very slight minority will follow the crowd exorcizing their frustrations and rebelliousness through socially acceptable channels. The desire to be accepted and respected for one's honesty and integrity supersedes the desire for riches and position acquired under the shadow of dishonesty and criminal cunning. The notion that man does not wish to behave honorable and decently, but does so solely out of fear, reduces him to the uncivilized stratum occupied by the animal.

The staunchest champions of "the system" are those who profit the most by it; the true criminal, the professional. For its design is such, that only the powerful, the wealthy, the cunning and the perverse can find shelter and succor within its confines; all others fall prey to its tyranny.

The intelligent and better informed take a different attitude. They readily admit the failure of the system and unhesitatingly point out its injustices and inequities; but in the final analysis they join forces with the multitude by refusing to encourage reform. To justify their passivity they take the apathetic position that while it obviously does not work and possesses some inhumane characteristics, it is all we have, therefore, it must be accepted.

Such complacency is the rule rather than the exception. It is this negligent attitude, rather than anything else that has retarded progress in the fields of criminology and penology, for it is only the intelligent and the informed who are capable of prodding the "establishment" into action. Sadly enough, those are the very people who having found their little niche in life, refuse to do anything which might jeopardize their comforts and security.

Others who are perhaps equally intelligent, but less informed have also carved out a comfortable place for themselves and guard it zealously. They have no desire to be better informed, in fact, they cherish their ignorance, for they suspect enlightenment could easily disturb the serenity of their lives or cause their comfort and security to become threatened. As long as they are not affected directly they are quite content to have others deal with their responsibilities for them. They feel this is a service they are paying for with their tax dollars, and having paid for the service they affect their righteous air of Pilate and proceed to wash their hands of the entire matter.

In recent years, the criminal justice system has been utilized as an instrument of chastisement and/or harassment against enemies of the establishment, or personal enemies of influential individuals and combines who retain a conspiratorial rapport with the power of established authority. In some instances it has become a weapon in the hands of unscrupulous politicians who employ it as a means of settling a private enmity and/or eliminating a potential threat to their position within the power structure. As a result, a few, who once may have enjoyed the comfort and security of the system, become ostracized, and more frequently victimized by it. They find themselves forced with the prospect of having to underwrite the cost of a lengthy and highly expensive legal battle. In some rare but noteworthy cases, their retribution has encompassed loss of social position, political obscurity, bankruptcy and imprisonment.

A wealth of magazine and newspaper articles have been written on the conditions in the jails and prisons. These institutions are painted in the most favorable hues and are reported to be as good, if not better, than most inmates are accustomed to enjoying in the free community. A perverse reasoning is employed here which relies upon exploiting the material and environmental poverty of the criminal. To a great extent, this is the prime motivation for the crime and authorities feebly attempt to justify the offender's failure to elevate his circumstances while he is imprisoned. The courts have been accused of coddling criminals and criticized for showing leniency or mercy, when in reality, the sentences they impose and the unethical method used in the process of adjudication are more criminal than any crime committed by the felon.

Rehabilitation propaganda is so grossly distorted as to offer a panacea, and beckons the "misfit" to come to prison, "where it's at".  All this camouflage to hide the actual situation giving society a resounding pat on the back for its patience, tolerance and charity in its dealings with the criminal belies and completely negates the supposed purpose of punishment.  For, as it has been noted, most are of the opinion that punishment acts as a deterrent to crime and espouses the belief that the severest penalty conceivable would eliminate crime, or at the very least, reduce it to a minimum.  When confronted by statistics that prove beyond doubt that punishment has no significant deterrent value with regard to the commission of crime.  They want to remedy this by advocating a "get tough" policy, which entails the use of greater punishments and less compassion.  This is reminiscent of the medieval theory that advocated "blood-letting" as a treatment for medical illness.  When a patient failed to respond favorable to the first bleeding the physician was convinced it was because he had neglected to relieve him or her of enough blood, whereupon he would proceed to bleed the patient again.  The majority so treated died, not from the disease or illness so much as from the loss of blood.  However, some did survive.  The same is true of the criminal justice system, some do survive its ministrations and go on to lead normal productive lives, not because of any treatment administered by the system, but very simply, in spite of it.

Some of those who, to attract attention, have employed bizarre and dramatically unorthodox means of exposing various injustices, inequities and inconsistencies within the established system of Government and State have been silenced through imprisonment.  The stigma of having served time in prison is enough to discredit an individual and serves to destroy the confidence of those who were or might have been influenced by him.  By the same token, the people who are now intimate with all aspects of the criminal justice system and who are eminently qualified to criticize or condemn it, have been reduced to a position of insignificance and their criticism or condemnation is interpreted as "sour grapes".  While this practice may temporarily silence the individual "free thinkers" and "non-conformists", it has some slight but nonetheless far-reaching consequences.  The cumulate effect of such an obviously tyrannical action, (coming at a time when the average American has become disenchanted, or at least mildly dissatisfied with the so-called "democratic process"), tends to weaken public confidence in the established order of things.  It also furnishes those foreign elements, who wish to completely undermine all democratic concepts, with a powerful instrument for fomenting national discontent and quasi-creditable provocation for insurgency.

People from all walks of life, clergymen as well as professionals in many fields, are joining forces with the proletariat to confront the establishment, seeking redress for their grievances; demanding to be made privy to the policies both foreign and domestic, that influence their lives; testing privileges they once assumed to be "rights" and investigating decadence and corruption within the bureaucracy.  The criminal justice system has managed to weather those storms of civic-consciousness perhaps a little better than some of the other less powerful agencies.  But the sometimes unethical maneuvering it manifests in retaining its sanctity renders it suspect.  These silent forces seeking to undermine our democracy are undoubtedly Communist inspired; however, they must have found a fertile breeding ground to have multiplied and survived the devastating onslaught of the opposing force of the democracy.

To the shallow intellect it may seem inconceivable that the most effective means of reducing the present day criminal justice system to a state of chaos and eventual destruction can be found within the constitution of the legislation which give it birth.  Yet, if one credits the creators of our system of justice with the wisdom and integrity required to conceive a process that provides the weak and the strong, the right and the poor, the guilty and the innocent, with equal protection and "due process of law", it must logically follow that they would incorporate into that system a self-destructive mechanism that would discourage corruption and miscarriage of justice.

Even though the Constitution guarantees that a person shall be presumed innocent until proven guilty, to the satisfaction of a jury made up of his peers, eighty-five to ninety percent of those accused of a crime ultimately surrender these basic rights, either through ignorance or coercion, by entering guilty pleas.  Still the courts are backlogged six to eight months and in some instances as much as eighteen months.  This condition infringes upon another Constitutional guarantee, the right to a speedy trial. If justice is to prevail, all Constitutional guarantees must be meticulously safeguarded by the courts that are entrusted with this task.  That the fundamental principles sustaining democracy are so  blatantly dismissed as mere formality, which can be waived by an  ignorant or intimidated defendant, or dispensed with by an  impatient or overburdened court is symptomatic of a malignancy within the system, which must be purged, with existing facilities and allotment of funds now available to the administrative branch of the criminal justice system, it is not difficult to see, that it would be physically as well as a financially impossibility to process every case in strict compliance with all the demands of Constitutional law.  Yet, every accused person has the unquestionable right to insist upon being so protected at every stage of the proceedings,  it is further guaranteed that he shall not be prejudiced, punished or held in contempt for doing so.  Therefore, if everyone, without exception, accused of a crime, were to plead "not guilty" and utilize all their resources as defined by and in strict accordance with the Articles of the Bill of Rights, exhausting every remedy to which they are entitled, the administrative branch of the criminal justice system would go bankrupt and collapse within a relatively short span of time.

Almost ninety percent of those who can afford bail and have the financial resources to employ competent legal representation enter "not guilty" pleas and stand trial are acquitted.  Less than ten percent of all indigents who are represented by court appointed counsel and stand trial win acquittal verdicts.  Better than eighty-five percent of those accused of crimes are declared indigents.  These figures, even if they were based on wild speculation (which they are not), indicate that crime is a behavior pattern which arises out of poverty.  Stated another way, it could be said that crime is an anti-social disease which is most prevalent among the poor and whose vaccine seems to be money. These same figures reveal the most significant reason for an illogically high percentage of guilty pleas.  A poor man only needs to be in custody for a few hours to realize his best and most expedient remedy is to be obtained through a docile wavering of all rights and surrendering himself to the oft times perfidious and seldom merciful ministration of the Courts.  He cannot envision the court as an unbiased and scrupulously just referee striving to make him equal under the laws, but a member of a hostile force, who, bent on extracting "a pound of flesh", demands supplication and placation from him.  The friend of the court, the public defender, is just another enemy forced on him, in the guise of an advocate, and more as a penance for his poverty.  He is as ill-equipped to face his day in Court as he has been to stand forth and meet the challenges of everyday living, in a society that imposes restriction and limitation based on economic status and origin of species, meanwhile ignoring its own moral obligations to pursue human understanding and promote brotherhood through loving and forgiving.

The character of our democracy in its original form was brought to life and nurtured in an environment of criminality, born out of frustration, by a  despot, who employed economic, social and cultural deprivation, to enslave the commoner and perpetuate a plutocratic order, whose benevolence and protection was limited to the Nobility.  In its infancy it epitomized the most cherished values of the oppressed, it was fashioned in a way that would, through a faithful adherence to its principles, finally expiate the crime.  It is sadly ironical that such a noble philosophy should become so adulterated as to begin to bear some of the intolerable traits of the force which motivated its conception.  The sins of criminal justice are the burdens of the democracy and represent the weakest link in the chain which anchors this Nation to humanity and its freedoms.  The boundaries separating plutocratic tyranny from capitalistic totalitarianism are indefinable.  If truth is to be found in mathematics, the equation that effects an indisputable balance would read:  capitalism plus totalitarianism equals crime, plus anarchy.

Recently the U. S. Supreme Court ruled the death penalty unconstitutional.  For a number of years it has been known that the death penalty was rarely carried out especially with the wealthy who were adjudged guilty of murder.  An infamous case in point that goes back many years were the killers of "Bobby Frank", Leopold and Loeb. These murderers were from wealthy families who acquired for their defense the greatest legal mind of the century, who, in spite of his clients" guilt, was able to get them off with life sentences. Many cases of more recent vintage could be cited to illustrate the same point. However, for the purpose of this discussion the above will suffice. With but few exception, it is the poor and the indigent who are asked to pay the supreme penalty. Because of their poverty, they are denied the same representation and protection as the rich. It has been pointed out here, that this same condition prevails, regardless of the seriousness of the crime. The sequence of events evident in most murders suggests that the victim is taken by surprise, he doesn't know that death is imminent, so there are no agonizing moments of anticipation which he must endure while waiting for his killer to act. To those who rely on sound logic to guide their reasoning, these last moments of conscious knowing are the pertinent aspects of the victims ordeal. Of death itself we know nothing, though we live with its very real presence in our daily lives. We cannot say with any degree of certainty, that it is the beginning of a new life, or simply the extinction of our consciousness. Be that as it may, a convicted killer who has been sentenced to death, if forewarned, he not only can anticipate the day and the hour, he will be executed, but the method that will be used to accomplish it. He must live with this knowledge on "death row" for many months and sometimes years, as in the case of Carol Chessman. In the interim he is given a realistic preview of his own last moments, as he watches others whose time has come, to walk or be carried the last mile, up those last thirteen steps to the chamber of death. It's impossible to imagine the horrors experienced daily by the inhabitants of "death row". Still there is a large segment of our society clamoring for legislation to reinstate this atrocious practice, on the premise that it acts as a deterrent to those who would commit murder.  Such an attitude must be considered perverse, especially in view of statistics that have been complied by States wherein the death penalty has been abolished, now for a number of years, which show no appreciable rise in murders since its abolition.

The crime of murder can never find justification or mitigation within the bounds of pure logic and sane reasoning.  A person, who fitfully takes a life, has to be extremely disorientated at the time he commits such an act.  Murder involves a state of mind which defies all logic and reason and will not be restored to sanity because of any consequences of its malfunctioning.  A good example of this can be found in an incident that took place in New York City, not long after the Supreme Court decision pertaining to capital punishment was publicized.  Two bank robbers were holding several people as hostages; they warned police, who had them surrounded, that unless they were permitted to escape they would not hesitate to kill all their captives; that since there was no longer a death penalty they had nothing to fear.  Even though the police shot and killed one of the bandits, the surviving would-be killer, failed to make good the threat and later released all the hostages unharmed.  Obviously these criminals had no intention of killing anyone, but upon finding themselves in an untenable position, decided to use as a psychological weapon to extricate themselves, an argument that had been planted in their minds by those who wish to have the death penalty returned.  Had their panic been extreme enough to temporarily derange them, resulting in the death of the hostages, those who formed this quasi-logical notion for them must surely have shared their guilt.  The one bandit already had been killed by police, how could surviving accomplice hope to be spared the same fate.  Only good sound reasoning stood in the way of the killing of the hostages.  The very fact that multiple murder did not materialize out of this particular set of circumstances seems to furnish a conclusive rebuttal to the argument that the death penalty acts as a deterrent regarding murder.

The questions which now plague the concerned citizen are:  Have we been acting outside the law all these years, condoning supposedly legal murder as a public service?  Why, has it taken the Supreme Court almost two centuries to decide that the death penalty is unconstitutional?

The Supreme Court no longer performs the function for which it was originally intended.  Nor, can it hope to do so, for it was set up at a time when the entire population of the Country numbered less than the present population of the city of Chicago.  Nine Justices had no difficulty hearing and ruling on all the cases submitted to them then, but it has now become a physical impossibility to give adequate perusal to as little as thirty percent of the cases submitted by a population that has swollen to forty times its original number.

A hearing before the U. S. Supreme Court is not, as some assume, a right, but a privilege which depends solely upon the discretionary powers of that court to grant or deny.  A person wishing to be heard by this august body, must first petition for permission to approach it.  This is no simple task, nor does the stringent abeyance to protocol and legal procedures end here.  All briefs must be submitted in printed form as prescribed by the Court.  To proceed in typewritten or handwritten form, one must obtain special permission from the Court, with but few exceptions, just enough to support the contention that the Court does not exercise discrimination or prejudice, certiorari is seldom granted to the indigent.  It will be found that approximately ninety-five percent of the cases granted certiorari were either, represented and/or supported by some socio-politic power group, or the case had attracted nationwide interest, or that the case was used as a vehicle for launching a socio-politic campaign of coercion against a State that has shown a stubborn refusal to acquiesce to the dictates of Federal Government.

In recent years, the Highest Court in the Land has degenerated into a political tool, whose primary function is the implementation of Federal domination over States Rights.  This becomes extremely evident when reviewing the adverse decisions it has handed down over the past two decades, against States that had displayed a steadfast endeavor to resist Federal intrusion upon their own sovereignty.  The lines which once indisputably separated State from Federal Government have been allowed to slowly erode through a simple but most effective process of repetitive and multi-phasic attach upon State Authority and jurisdiction, culminating in decisions which constantly narrow their power to govern.

Through the past three or four administrations which have ranged over a broad spectrum, from the ultra-liberal to the middle of the road conservatism, the court has undergone some unprecedented and suspicious changes in character and talent.  Few questioned the reasons why one Justice enjoyed such a brief stay or why such a comparatively young and brilliant appointee of a purported ultra-liberal administration, should suddenly resign the second highest appointed office in the land, to accept a somewhat obscure position with the United Nations, when the policies of leadership began to reflect a conservative ideology.  What premature retirement or resignation from this all powerful court can escape the concerned inquiry of a politically neutral commission?  Few had the wisdom or intelligence to grasp the full significance of the "Warren

Commission", or heard in it the death knell of a "just" democracy which reverberated throughout the world.

The "Law" in all its ambiguous verbosity has become meaningless. It has been written and rewritten, phrased and rephrased, ruled upon and then ruled upon again many times over. The once clearly defined boundaries of its authority and jurisdiction have through repetitious legislation and interpretation vanished. It has now become dependent upon the temperament, prejudices and eccentricities of the individual jurist responsible for its administration. Court records will disclose adjudication that is variable, if not, shamefully contradictory, within the same Court by the same Judge and in many instances within the same term of court on issues, both matter of fact and "matter of record", which clearly fall under identical legal circumstances, for which precedents have already been established, both contrary to and in agreement with any decision rendered. These ambiguities are not confined to the law in general terms but have eaten their way into the nucleus of its being, for even the legal definition of words within its text have been changed, through Court interpretation, to the point where they have lost the basic substance of their original connotation.

Because of a Supreme Court decision, handed down in the late fifties, the word "stolen", no longer means, something which is taken without the owners knowledge or consent and for the express purpose of permanently depriving him of his property. In the case of U. S. vs. Turley, the Court ruled that the word stolen as it appears in the Dyer Act is to be taken in its broader sense, that is, it must now encompass fraud, intent to defraud and fraudulent conversion. This was a 5 to 4 decision where the dissenting opinion severely takes the majority to task for their presumption in assuming a responsibility which belongs to

Congress. The dissenters argued that since the Congress had repeatedly refused to change the wording of the Dyer Act, which was under their consideration at three previous sessions, the Supreme Court was acting outside its authority and jurisdiction when it contravened the intent of the congressional body. This is not an isolated case where the entire meaning and intent of the law has been changed by the courts interpretation of its language, but rather a good illustration of the distortion and degeneration that prevails throughout the system.

One very pointed example of the duplicity evinced in legal terminology through interpretation can be found in the famous landmark decision Gideon vs. Wainwright, (it may be appropriate to observe here that this decision, which threw the criminal justice system of the State of Florida into a turmoil and caused that State considerable expense and embarrassment to accommodate, was handed down at a time when it was exhibiting a stubborn refusal to subordinate itself to Federal domination). On the surface, this decision seems to clearly impart the rights of the ignorant and the indigent to be represented, and to be heard, no matter how feeble the cry for help or how decrepit the vehicle used to transport the issue into the court room. Yet, there obviously exists enough ambiguity or flexibility within its text to permit the courts to continue to ignore any petitions from indigents unfamiliar with proper court procedures, who lack the necessary knowledge, ability and skill, to prepare a sophisticated legal petition. It is still common practice for some courts to refuse to acknowledge handwritten letters, which are obviously intended as legal petitions, from indigents who have no other means of communicating their grievance. This is especially true in cases where the petitioners are incarcerated. From the standpoint of the prisoner, it would appear that his ignorance, poverty and imprisonment are being exploited, to deny him "equal protection and due process of law".

Many find that even though their petitions are acknowledged and docketed, the Courts will either arbitrarily deny them or forestall and delay disposition via permitting the prosecutor to indulge in legalistic intrigues. Most eventually despair of acquiring relief and withdraw their petitions. The more persistent litigant, who has the patience to see things through, may find himself still endeavoring to be heard at the expiration of his sentence.

The wheels of justice are fluid and swift when the issue to be decided represents a threat to authority or has socio-politic overtones. However, when the issue involved the grievance of an insignificant indigent, they move in a laboriously ponderous fashion. When it is pointed out that the poor and friendless are denied equal protection and due process of law, society will treat inequity in a pseudo-philosophical fashion; the attitude being: "The system is far from perfect, but it's the best one in the world".

The Courts are physically enveloped in a theatrically staged atmosphere of righteous dignity and omnipotence, expressly designed to intimidate and coerce those who fall prey to their influence and judgment.

Local attorneys who have gained the reputation as "fixers" come by it honestly and work diligently to maintain that status, for this is the talent that permits them to command exorbitant fees and sets them in a class above the "hacks" in their profession, who have failed to make the right contacts. All rely on their ability to retain a conspiratorial rapport with various Judges and Prosecutors, to insure their continued success. Not having to practice law, in the practical sense, few are capable lawyers, but each in his own peculiar way, is a past master at political intrigue. It is not unusual to discover, at a lunch time recess, the main participants (Judge, Prosecutor, and Defense Attorney) in the same litigation, drinking and dining together at a local club, cocktail lounge or restaurant. Bridge partners, political partisans, habitual companions at social functions, intimate friends and confidants, become hostile protagonists, when representing opposing forces in the court room. Under normal circumstances people who form close and lasting alliances in all other areas of living, cannot become arch enemies, casting aside allegiance and confidence without upsetting the balance of the entire relationship. Obviously one of the faces these people present to the world is a mask; and it is not difficult to mark the distinction.

Where there are "fixers" there also exists a situation that can easily be exploited by the adventurers in the legal profession. These are usually lawyers who in reality have no connections whatsoever; they couldn't fix a parking ticket. Still they approach a frightened and naïve prospective client with a swaggering, self-confidence, that is reassuring, while they are at best mediocre attorneys or at best, master con-artists who have developed the knack of making the client feel secure in the knowledge that he is in capable hands. Some are so glib that they often succeed in convincing a thoroughly experienced client of their proprietorship to legal powers and influential connections. Those who have acquired a polished style, in this type intrigue, refrain from making concrete promises or positive statements. Through innuendo and insinuation they convince their "dupe" that the stage is set, but piously refuse to betray professional confidences by divulging details. All that is required of the client is money and cooperation. As a rule, the client of one of these clever but supremely unscrupulous counselors seldom realizes what has happened to him until sometime after he has been committed to a prison.

It has been a long established practice for a defense lawyer to "bargain" or "deal" with prosecutors, who in turn act as liaison between the Judge and the defense. Sometimes an attorney has enough influence with a Judge, so that the "Middleman" can be dispensed with. Bargaining is not only profitable (legalized bribery, which permits a defendant capable of doing so, to purchase a share of justice,) for the Judges, prosecutors and defense attorneys, but can in many cases, save the State and the Court a great deal of time and money. While it does have certain advantages, (for the defense and the Courts, a condition prevails which can and often does permit a guilty defendant, (provided he has sufficient financial resources) to purchase his freedom or leniency. More often it is responsible for extreme punitive measures being levied against the indigent, who is incapable of paying for his share of justice. Many times defense attorneys will throw two or three of their clients, (who are usually in no position to pay legal fees, and for whom the attorneys, were court appointed) to the wolves, in order to make the best deal for a wealthy client. Many times the prosecutor's case against a defendant is so weak, the cooperation of his defense lawyer is enlisted by the State to insure a conviction. If he hopes to keep the door open for future "bargaining and dealing", he must do as he is told. Basically what bargaining amounts to is the "trading" of one person's freedom, for that of another. Here the people, whose lives are being used as a medium of exchange, have lost all identity as human beings and the practice is performed in a grotesquely impersonal and callous fashion.

If the Law is to retain the respect of the community, most especially that segment of it which is potentially criminal, it must perform its office honestly, courteously and legally. It cannot owe its success or failure to methods or practices that are morally or legally unethical. This may sound much too idealistic to be practical; however, this is not an area in which idealism can in any way be sacrificed for the sake of practicality. The slightest deviation from a religious adherence to moral principles, should nullify any claim the system may have for its justification. This is not a situation where the end can at any time justify the means. Crime is crime irregardless of its costume and irrespective of the socio-politic status of the one committing the act. To embrace crime as a means of dealing with or combating crime is to encourage and compound it.

When the Supreme Court finally ruled that police must inform a suspect of his right to remain silent and to be represented by counsel, during interrogation by them, many objections were raised. Not only did these objections emanate from the police, but society also joined in to denounce the decision. Such a reaction readily identifies the attitudes of both.

Police naturally disdained this edict, because it made their job a trifle more difficult. Now they would be required to defend their own industry and intelligence to gather enough factual physical evidence to connect a suspect with a crime, something which the law really required them to do all along. No longer could they rely upon the use of brute force and coercion to deprive a citizen of his rights to the presumption of innocence. In theory, police are now restrained from menacingly converging on a suspect in a dark, and unsanitary cell especially designed to frighten and intimidate him and by the use of physical torture and fear, force him to stand trial in their own private court without legal assistance or succor. In reality, though the methods have been somewhat refined and are less crudely applied, the practice still persists and is nonetheless effective.

Society's attitude is not as easily identified or understood unless one reflects back to biblical times and considers the primitive psychology manifested by the multitude.  Christ was condemned to death, by crucifixion, through a similar kind of logic which underlies the reasoning that has interpreted this decision to signify that it will permit the guilty to go free, and supports the contention that the Courts are coddling the criminal.  It is doubtful that such an attitude could, through any set of circumstances be justifiable, but if justification were to be made plausible, a large portion of the constitution would have to be rewritten. If nothing else, the attitude of society vividly demonstrates the need for constitutional law and supplies mute testimony to the wisdom of its authors.

From the moment of arrest and for as long as he is subjected to the over-powering authority of the criminal justice system, an individual experiences intimidation or coercion, in some for or another.  Coercion can assume many disguises.  It can be crudely physical or subtly mental. Insofar as every day application of this method of persuasion, the average offender, viewing his experience in retrospect, usually finds he has at some time or other been introduced to and victimized by just about every facet of the diabolical art of coercion.

Even though a suspect is apprehended on a warrant, charging him with a non-violent crime, he learns to anticipate a certain amount of man-handling, ill-treatment and abuse from the arresting officers, who seem to perform their duties with a sadistic zealousness. Part of this show of force and penchant toward cruelty is displayed when he is rudely thrust against the side of a building or in some cases over the hood of an automobile, hand over head, feet well away from the supporting structure, the legs are spread apart sometimes with the none-too gentle caress of a club or the muzzle of a loaded police revolver.  He is then searched, often with unnecessary brutality, in the more delicate parts of the body.  Although the search is thorough and reveals no hidden weapon, the hands are generally manacled, (sometimes so securely that circulation is cut off or the skin is broken) behind his back.  He is then shoved or pushed inside a waiting police van or patrol car for the uncomfortable and off times painful ride to the police station.

Once inside the privacy of the station house, the suspect's captors are free to indulge their sadistic instincts without fear or interruption or censure.  Here a suspect is "toyed with" in much the same disgusting manner, as a cat might be observed playing with a mouse, before it finally tires of the sport and destroys it.  He is stripped not only of clothing but of his dignity.

When a suspect is "bound over" for grand jury action, bail is set.  Bail set in Magistrates Court, is, as a rule, ridiculously high and completely out of reach for the indigent.  Being unable to post bail a suspect is removed from the city "lockup" and transported to the County jail, where food rations, cell accommodations and conditions in general are not the best.  Prisoners are celled together indiscriminately; the young with the old; the semi-sane with the demented; the sex-deviate with the murderer; the con-artist with the bank robber, etc.  A hodgepodge of social-misfits, whose confinement has been arranged, as a safety precaution, to protect society; all gather together within the same compound.  Jail personnel and guard forces are primarily concerned with security, (that is, keeping the inmates confined) and are inadequately staffed and unable to control or properly police the internal situation. Consequently, crime inside the jail is commonplace and ranges in seriousness, from petty theft and simple assault to rape and murder.

In jail, everything has a price and nothing is unobtainable. The prisoner who can afford it can elevate his standard of living. The items which can be purchased are revealing, in that they tend to call attention to the things which are denied the average prisoner. Purchasable items are: private cells, sheets, pillows, pillowcases, innerspring mattresses, clothing, food (from outside restaurants or home) fresh fruit, furniture, rugs, newspapers, books, magazines, radios, TV's, recorders and record players, medical and dental care, medication and funeral trips and bedside visits to dying relatives.

Another factor which contributes to the perpetuation of the present system, is that jailors, prison guards and police, like their charges, are ill-suited for healthy social-integration. Perhaps, the best thing that can be said of the system is, that it provides a place for these defective personalities permitting them to lead comparatively normal lives in a society where they could not possibly survive or gain acceptance otherwise. The healthy well-adjusted person who accidentally gets involved with the criminal justice system, is repelled and appalled by what he sees and divorces himself from it at the earliest possible moment.

It is doubtful if anyone who has not served a year or more, as an inmate, inside a penitentiary, could imagine what it is like. Imprisonment is a traumatic experience of such magnitude as to permanently scar the mind, the body and the spirit. The conglomerate composition of its populace epitomizes humanity at its vilest stage of depravity. To adjust to this environment is to adopt its deformities. In the prison community kindness is taken for weakness and polite consideration is considered effeminate. Petty intrigue, duplicity and informing, offer the best and most expedient avenues for gaining favor with prison officials, who can influence parole boards, and contribute immeasurably to the comfort and security of the inmate. Prison administrators never lack for bait to dangle before an inmate, when his cooperation is needed to insure the successful operation of the Institution.

Because the population of the prisons are less transient than that of local jails, conditions of necessity are healthier and more sanitary. The routine is regimented and the police unit maintains a better quality of discipline and order.

Psychotics are given the run of the Institutions, either because the prison psychiatrist (where there is one) and/or officials are incapable of recognizing their danger to other inmates or, deliberately ignore them, rather than transfer them to mental institutions where they can be given adequate treatment and kept under control. It is not uncommon to see an inmate who has been acting strangely, suddenly become violent and attack another inmate for no apparent reason. Bullies and active perverts are permitted to prey upon the weaker and less aggressive type inmate. Much of this is the result of inadequate supervision or a collusive relationship between guards and the aggressors. In other cases the guard may have a physical handicap, a cowardly streak or be too old and frail to intercede. Rather than get involved in an incident which might very well call attention to his incapacity, he will turn his back on a situation. Twenty years ago, assault on a prison guard or official was almost unheard of. For the punishment, regardless of the provocation, dire consequences could result in the inmate being crippled for life or beaten to death. Prison guards and officials alike have now become especially wary of Blacks, who are getting a measure of protection from "Rights Groups" and pro-black organizations.

To offset their permissiveness and tolerance to Blacks, which has tended to undermine their power of authority, guards are prone to single out the more docile and timid white prisoners for disciplining, with more frequency and less justification.

The flow of contraband in prisons is more rigidly controlled than it is in the local jails, but this is not to say it is unavailable.  Some state prisons are notorious for their traffic in contraband.  This is especially true of those institutions that still permit inmates to possess "outside" or "free world" currency.

Despite the better quality of discipline and tighter security inside the prisons, crime is as prevalent there as it is in the jails.  The higher risk factor, coupled with the threat of being given additional time to serve, tends to encourage the use of an unusual amount of stealth and cunning, in the commission of a prison crime.  As a result, crime inside the prison is almost always of a serious nature, the repercussions of which envelop the victim as well as the perpetrator.

The homogenization of all different types of offenders, forms the character of the prison and exerts a lasting detrimental influence on the inmate.  What few principles the individual inmate has managed to retain become hopelessly corrupt, in this environment.  An unsophisticated offender is introduced to a wide variety of crimes and methods of accomplishing them.  Bitterness, resentment and frustration is engendered, and grows in proportion to the abuses and injustices inflicted upon the prisoner by the prison system itself, without exception all inmates suffer from paranoia to some degree.  Rather than providing a stimulus for emotional and mental maturation, prison retards it.  The system itself is constantly striving to emasculate the criminal; as a substitute it offers homosexuality or physical and mental vegetation. Feelings of impotency and despair become so pronounced as to induce masochism, acute schizophrenia and in some cases dementia praecox. Those who are considered by prison officials as well adjusted inmates have surrendered their individuality, personality and free will and have become reliant upon the system to do their thinking for them. Many inmates after serving several years in prison, are totally institutionalized and are incapable of making even the most rudimentary kind of an adjustment to the "free world". Tensions and anxieties mount as the release date approaches. The closer an inmate gets to release, the more apprehensive he becomes, subconsciously he fears freedom, for with it comes the responsibility for himself; that has always been his nemesis. It may sound unreasonable or illogical to say that the prison has an irresistible appeal to the released inmate, but this is actually the case. For just as the heroin addict has developed a physical and psychological dependence upon the drug which has demoralized and dehumanized him, so has the prisoner developed an addiction to the prison that has extracted a similar toll of his personality.

The moral values and behavior standards of the criminal have been undergoing a slow process of deterioration and decay for some time. Imprisonment, rather than halting this decaying process or neutralizing the acids that are corroding the terminals which link the individual to society, serve merely to hasten his moral and social demise. While the immediate social problems created by the criminal have been temporarily solved through his incarceration, a much more serious problem is being fermented in the demonical cauldron of the prison, which will prove exceedingly more difficult to cope with once he is returned to the free community.

Here again statistics disclose an inexcusable and tragic situation. The percentage of repeated offenders is staggering. Official sources admit that three out of every four criminals committed to prison return within ten years; better than eighty percent of these are re-imprisoned within the first six months after being released.

Over the past fifty or sixty years, the prison system has supposedly undergone a series of reforms. It has just passed through the "rehabilitation" stage and is now entering into a new phase that is grounded upon the premise that only the young first offender is salvageable. With this new theory the emphasis is on youth. The recidivist, who was once a youthful first offender himself and is now the finished product of an abortive experiment, is unceremoniously "dumped" into the "garbage can", and it's back to the drawing board for new plans. So then with one fell-swoop, the system washes its own slate clean at the expense of many thousands of lives. The new technique is quietly implemented and the fanfare and publicity usually engaged in when some progressive innovation has been incorporated in the system, is conspicuously absent. The reason for this is obvious to the older recidivist, for if it were openly acknowledged it would pave the way to a class action, which could free those who are discriminated against, and are being left to stagnate for want of therapy. In addition, the Courts refuse to consider the fact that the repeat offender, if sentenced to prison today, goes there but for one purpose only and this is punishment; they refuse to consider that the treatment programs he had been exposed to in the past were defective and may have conceivably contributed to his recidivism. Under the circumstances, a just court should judge the repeat offender with more tolerance than ever before, for, in reality, it is now being asked to pass judgment upon the end product of a defunct method, which must certainly share the burden for the criminals release.  Not only has the recidivist served as a human guinea-pig for an unsuccessful experiment, that has permanently deformed him, he is also saddled with the responsibility and blame for its failures and is punished more severely because of it.

Sentence imposed rarely bears a reasonable relationship to the crime from which they issue.  An automobile thief, charged with one count of auto larceny, will be given a five year prison sentence, while a bank officer, who has been charges with embezzling several thousand dollars, will be admonished, fined five hundred dollars and placed on a year's probation.  A man charged with forging a fifty-dollar check and causing it to be transported interstate, is sentenced to ten years in prison by the same Court that apologetically sentences an armed bank bandit to an hour in the custody of the marshal (odd sounding, but true).

When sentences are not fixed or mandatory, the responsibility for determining punishment is surrendered to the discretion of the Court and conditions exist which encourage injustice and precludes a uniformly impartial judgment.  Every crime, without exception, embraces a certain amount of extenuating and mitigating factors. Recognizing them requires insight into the personality and circumstances of the offender.  Bringing them to bear in the best interest of the accused, at the time of judgment, involves the intelligence and skill of a thoroughly experienced attorney.  Unfortunately, the average offender enjoys very little insight into himself, or, when he does realize his motivations he has too much shame or misplaced pride to divulge them.  Nor is he financially able to pay a capable attorney, in whom he can confide and depend upon to enlist the Court's understanding and compassion.

Some years ago, a judiciary committee gave serious consideration to an "average sentence law". Had it been acted upon and passed, it would have eliminated the disparity in sentences that exists today. Sentences would have been fixed to terms that would not have exceeded the average time that was served by past offenders for all crimes. But after studying the bill more closely the committee decided to reject it, for it was discovered that if it was endorsed and passed into law, many of the crimes which are now held to be felonies would have to be reduced to misdemeanor status, entailing a complete overhaul of the laws and the courts.

As things now stand, Federal laws overlap State laws and punishment for these duplications are asymmetrical. Seriousness of crimes vary from State to State, Court to Court and Magistrate to Magistrate, as do sentencing statutes. What is treated as a felony in one court may well be considered a misdemeanor in another. Though for all practical purposes the buying power of the dollar has been reduced by two-thirds its face value, the amount required to constitute grand larceny still stands at the unrealistic figure of one hundred dollars, in a few states, while others refuse to extend the amount beyond the fifty or seventy-five dollar limit.

Previous record is a prime consideration to the courts, at the time they are making a determination of the sentence. Not only is this an unjust practice, it is undeniably contemptuous of the "double jeopardy clause" of the Constitution. When a sentence is originally imposed, it must be understood that all pertinent factors relative to the crime have been deliberated once and for all, and that the punishment has been custom-tailored to suit the circumstances present. Once that particular sentence has been served, the criminal has paid the price demanded of him and should not be subjected to additional injury or judgment, beyond that which was stipulated.  If the courts insist upon weighting a previous offense on the same scale with the present one, it must afford the accused the right to defend himself and since he has already paid the penalty asked of him, his defense is well established.

Little thought is given to the multi-faceted and enduring handicaps that accompany conviction of a criminal offense.  Once imprisoned the individual is forever branded. The stigma hangs over a man like an ominous cloud, clinging to him with a relentless tenacity.  It discourages ambition, engenders a withdrawal from healthy social intercourse, compromises principles and invites subterfuge. The most honorable aims and intentions of the ex-convict are suspect, in view of remembered transgressions that place him in a position where he is always at the mercy of his co-workers and neighbors.

In spite of the fact that the Johnson administration spent several million dollars to compile the findings and recommendations of a Crime commission study, few, if any of its recommendations were adopted.  The commission condemned the policies and practices of the Parole Boards and recommended that present methods for determining parole status be abolished, on the premise that parole should not be looked upon as a privilege, but should be the right of everyone serving a sentence in our prisons.  A right which could not be forestalled or forfeited by anything short of a serious breach of prison regulations.

The powers of the parole boards are practically limitless and the law regulating its authority is so broad, it might just as well have never been written.  In addition to having to face the judgment of the court, a sentenced prisoner must also submit to a subsequent judgment by the

Parole Board, which invariably holds a longer tenure of authority over him then the sentencing court.

Paroles are granted on a highly discriminatory and prejudicial basis. Although an individual's previous record is taken into consideration by the courts at the time of sentencing, the parole board judges him again on that basis when making its own determination. While parole authorities lay claim to granting paroles to around thirty-percent of the prison population annually, it does not bother to break this figure down into groups to show how many were first offenders, or how many were multi-offenders; nor does it show what percentage has served beyond or how far beyond their eligibility date, before this action was taken. Of the thirty percent the parole board claims to have paroled, it is estimated that less than seven percent are repeat offenders and since seventy-five percent of the prisons population is made up of inmates in that category, parole has little, if any, validity for the majority.

Where the possibility of parole is present and the law does not allow the sentencing courts to impose or infringe upon the authority of the parole boards in determining parole status, the court must either anticipate the action of the parole boards, or assume that everyone will be paroled, provided they conform to prison regulations and make satisfactory adjustments in the prison community.

It can be argued that what has been written here up to this point, is biased and grossly distorted assessment of the conditions that actually exist, aimed at relieving the criminal of guilt and placing the blame for this failure to respond to the ministration of the system upon society or the system itself. Yet, it cannot be denied that the criminal's behavior goes from "bad" to "worse" under the guidance, treatment and influence of a system over which he has no control or voice in formulating. If the sincerity of the author's efforts to develop the criminal's point of view in hopes of bringing about constructive changes that will benefit society, as well as the criminal, is taken in good faith which manifests itself, via open mind, and which acknowledges the failure of the present system, the need to defend it vanishes.  Or, if the system is undeserving of criticism, no defense is required.

The picture formed thus far is rendered in generalities which depict the peripheral influences of the criminal justice system upon the criminal.  Other than having labeled the average criminal a "bonafide" mental case, his defects have not been discussed.  However, at this point, before going into that problem, one further observance is in order and must be evaluated and given a measure of consideration. Since the close of World War II and very noticeably since the 1954 Supreme Court decision on "Civil Rights" the ethnic character of the nation's prisons have been undergoing an unprecedented change.

In the forties and up into the early fifties, the ethnic population of the jails and prisons coincided with the ethnic composition of the free community.  That is to say, the bulk of the prisoners were white, about ninety percent, while blacks and other ethnic minorities made up the remaining ten percent.  Today, however, blacks account for better than sixty percent of the jail and prison populace of the United States.  In some of the larger urban jail facilities, that figure climbs to better than ninety percent.  Once those figures are thoroughly digested, it appears as though a good sixty percent of the more serious crime is being committed by a poverty ridden, underprivileged and socially deprived ethnic group and brings home the fact that these seem to be the same basic factors present in almost all crime, regardless of the ethnic origin of the criminal.  Now, the question arises, are blacks actually responsible for committing sixty percent of the nation's crime or is imprisonment being used as a means of intimidating blacks into assuming a submissive role in our society?  If it is found that the former is true and that a group of people who represent a mere ten percent of our total population, have become law breakers, then serious thought must be given to dealing with insurgency.  There is a bottomless chasm separating the domestic criminal from the insurgent.  Insurgents should be singled out, acknowledged as political prisoners and entitled to the rights of the politico militant, while in custody and segregation from ordinary criminals, if for no other reason than to protect those who are identified by the revolutionaries as being affiliated with the enemy.  Very little can be accomplished in the field of criminology until this issue is clarified and resolved.  If the prisons are being used to detain revolutionaries, the atmosphere will become intolerable for all concerned and a gradual break down of order and discipline will result in producing a climate of unrest.  This would preclude a favorable response to treatment.

The confined offender has, at one time or another, been used as a human guinea-pig to facilitate scientific research.  Although he has been the subject for several unsuccessful experiments in penology, he has never been subjected to a microscopic analysis to determine whether the origin of his damaged thinking faculties could be traced to an organic or chemical malfunction.  Likewise, there has been relatively no recent comprehensive, scientific study made of the thinking processes of the criminal mind.  Perhaps the latter is excusable on the grounds that to really know and understand the offender, the scientist would necessarily have to live with him on a twenty-four hour a day basis, over a period of many months or even years.

A marked example of the lack of scientific expertise in the area  of criminology, and one which characterizes the ignorance and naiveté of  science in its efforts to solve the offender's problems, can be found in the rehabilitation theory.  Though science may be dealt an injustice here, it is quite possible that this abortion may have taken seed in the bureaucratic labyrinth and then managed to acquire a tolerant nod from the scientific world.  To think in terms of rehabilitation is to pre-suppose that an individual was, at one time habilitated.  A mere cursory glance at the average criminal's history should convince even the layman that habilitation was never effected.  Proceeding on that premise, it doesn't require a professionally trained and scientific mind to realize that rehabilitation will place the offender right back where he started, namely, upon the threshold of crime where his degeneration started.  Despite the record of utter failure accredited to rehabilitation methods, the system steadfastly refuses to admit to error and fixes the blame for its own shortcomings upon the offender.  One of its weakest excuses can be found in its favorite contention that a person must first want to be rehabilitated for the method to succeed.  What the offender needs and desperately wants is not rehabilitation but "habilitation".

Some prisons have special units for housing new inmates awaiting processing and classification.  While in this unit, the inmates are introduced to the prison routine by means of a series of orientation lectures given by various officers who represent the institution's administration.  A few years ago, a favorite topic for one of these lectures was the institution's rehabilitation program.  Today, however, one hears a brief and negatively intoned reference to this method.  The new inmate is bluntly informed, "no one is going to wave a magic wand over you here."  Or, "we can't rehabilitate you, this is something you must do for yourself."

It takes a courageous or highly insensitive prison official to stand up before a group of prisoners today and mention the word "rehabilitate" even in a facetious manner.

The term "rehabilitation" is used to describe a supposedly progressive method of treating the convicted offender. Its predecessors were the "correction" and "reform" methods. The word "rehabilitate" means, "to restore to condition of health or useful and constructive activity."

The word "reform" is synonymous with the word "correct", meaning "to amend or improve by change of form or removal of faults or abuses". In connection with the offender, the word "reform" describes a method better calculated to deal with the problem realistically, provided of course that it subordinates all other considerations and is used as the dominating focal point of the entire program. The offender must be taken out of his isolation and introduced to the world of reality and like a child he must be given a knowledgeable and trusted guide who will reshape his values. In the process he must also be supplied with the tools that will equip him to realize his true capacities and the ability to see himself in logical perspectives that remain consistent with his capabilities and potentials. To complete his education, he must be taught the necessity of accepting his situation.

The success of such a program, entails intensive therapy, the greater portion of which needs to be pursued on a personal and individual level, within an atmosphere that is conclusive to producing in him a desire for change.

Taking an unemotional assessment of the various methods devised to correct criminal behavior (an error which seems to consistently repeat itself), is the starting point of each theory. By the laborious process of following the stream of logic to its headwater, one invariably finds the

source of the flow to emanate from an underground spring, the water of which, is discolored and tainted by the characteristics of a basically evil, dishonest and sub-human species. Here seems to be the major stumbling block, for in reality, with the possible exception of his retarded development, the criminal is much like everyone else. His aims are on a par with the average, normal individual; namely, that he is desirous of obtaining a reputation for honesty, industry and
of belonging and acceptance, etc. The difference between the offender and the well adjusted individual is that he hasn't the remotest idea of how he should go about acquiring those desires in an orthodox manner. He has never learned to cope with the simple ordinary problems of a sophisticated and highly complex society. An everyday problem which may represent an interesting challenge to the normal individual, develops into a major crisis when confronting the offender. Subjected to the pressures of the most uncomplicated mode of living the criminal has a tendency to panic, distorting and disrupting his ability to reason logically. In most instances he is guided not by sound reasoning but rather he becomes completely dominated by his emotionally immature attitudes.

In the healthy person, reason and logic, while being intimidated to some degree by the emotions, maintain their dominion in governing human behavior. Genetics may be credited with supplying the basic substance of the emotions but the mind itself is responsible for emotional philology by the process of receiving, digesting and interpreting the impressions it perceives from the outside environment. By the same token, the mind that may harbor hereditary defects of an inorganic nature, can repair itself if exposed to the proper and appropriate environmental elements. The critical stage of development comes at a time when the mind and emotions are still in a malleable state which will be molded by information that is transmitted through the senses forming the basis for all the thought and sensation patterns that subsequently develop.  When development does not progress along a normal course, nature, by virtue of its wisdom in assuming a slow pace toward fixed evolution of the personality, provides ample opportunity for correcting any defects while the individual is still in the developmental stage.  However, the need for correction must not only be perceived, but intelligently applied.  Few parents are equipped to perform unemotionally or intelligently in either area, so that when correction is needed and effected, it is, as a rule, the result of chance accompanied by a propitious set of circumstances.  Unfortunately, neither of these elements were present to assist in the development of the criminal, nor are corrective aids made available to him in the community of the prison.

No two people are exactly alike; therefore, none are exactly equal.  True maturity, or more accurately, complete habilitation, can be measured by the individual's ability to accurately assess and then willingly accept his own limitations within the boundaries prescribed by his emotional development.  Though one man may be as intelligent, skilled or as talented as another, the emotional factor inevitably intervenes to affect an imbalance.  The average, well adjusted person has a fairly good estimate of his own worth in regard to others, and expects no more of life than he is entitled to; nor is he plagued by frustrations that could annoy him if he had set goals for himself that were beyond his reach.  The offender hasn't the remotest idea what his actual capabilities and potentialities are, and his is likewise incapable of evaluating others.  He is swayed by superficial elements and attaches prime significance of worth to material possessions and position.  Those who enjoy a normal pattern of development have learned that each man has his limitations which demand of him an uncompromising recognition and conciliation.  Those who never learn this basic truth are destined to go through life frustrated and maladjusted.  In the criminal offender this frustration has become so severely acute as to hopelessly cripple his ability to employ sound reason as well as undistorted logic to guide his judgment.  That his maladjustment has manifested itself in the form of criminal behavior can be attributed to accident more than to any premeditated design on his part.  However, once the pressures of his emotional illness find that outlet, a new pattern is established which in time becomes as ingrained as all the others until it has formed a permanent bond with his personality.

The degeneration and disorientation process that began in the free community, in lieu of habilitation, ripens into full maturity under the cumulative influences of the criminal justice system.  It is unrealistic to presume, that the offender, who is already badly warped and seriously disorientated, will respond in a positive way to a system that possesses such an overwhelming preponderance of negative stimuli.  Adjustment to a completely foreign condition of living, as opposed to that of the free community, and one from which there is no alternative or escape, is forced upon the criminal.  Like a dose of castor oil given to a child complaining of bellyache, he cringes and recoils from it, for he knows its very odor will cause him to retch; and society, like the old fashioned parent who knows what is best, holds his nose and forces it down his gullet.  It is only logical to reason that once he becomes acclimated and makes a satisfactory adjustment to the prison community, it will be virtually impossible for him to make a healthy or stable transition to any other type of environment in the absence of similar inducements, restraints and perpetual guidance.

It is difficult to imagine the effects of the system upon one as already warped as the criminal. It may better facilitate comprehension to visualize the changes that would take place in a normal well adjusted person when exposed to similar conditioning. The John Dillingers and Charles Mansons are isolated cases, merely because of unfortunate circumstances which prevented them from being apprehended before they were able to extract their own share of vengeance from a society which chose to cultivate their illness and aggravate it, rather than treat it.

A person who has been unable to manage his life outside of prison is considered to be acclimatized to prison life and in a sense it has become a refuge. He is given a very uncomplicated roadmap for living on the outside with a policeman on every corner to give him directions and prevent him from making any serious errors in judgment. Once he surrenders his independence and permits himself to be swept along with the tide, life becomes uncomplicated and a certain degree of comfort and security ensues. He is so enraptured with this new feeling of security and respite from the turmoil of trying to cope with living, that he acquires an addiction to prison, and before he realizes it, it has cost him his individuality and freedom. He soon awakens to the realization that he is a mere shell of a man, a vegetable, incapable of relating to people and things outside the prison environment. By this time he has regressed to the point where he is emotionally impotent and mentally sterile.

Though the popular belief is that we have come a long way and made much progress in the treatment of criminals, the truth of the matter is that we have made relatively few fundamental changes. "Punishment" is still the prime objective; and "Imprisonment" still acts as the implement utilized to accomplish it. It is of little consequence to the criminal offender today, that he has escaped being chained to an oar in the hold of a prison ship, for he realizes that he is just as securely shackled, in a physical as well as a mental sense, to a system that generates in him the same degree of despair and hopelessness experienced by his counterparts of centuries gone by.  The changes that have been made and heralded as progress were nothing more than semantic refinements of old and long established practices and concepts.

While the criminal in his present state is a bonafide mental case, his mental facilities are not so deranged as to defy reconstruction or repair.  In fact, he is of a group that has exhibited an encouragingly healthy response to psycho-therapy when it has been conscientiously administered by competent dedicated professionals.

The science of psychiatry is still in its infancy; and its success and progress has been limited to the treatment of personality disorders and minor mental derangements of an inorganic nature.  Therefore, assuming the offender's disability stems from an inorganic cause, he falls well within the scope of scientific progress in the field of psychiatry and deserves to be given the benefit of its cognizance and knowledge.  By similar reasoning, society has the right to demand priority in the utilization of the latest advancements in all scientific areas, and a moral obligation to humanity to make them available to those who can benefit by them. However, for this approach to succeed, the entire problem of criminality must be attacked with scientific discipline and strategy.  The generals should be master tacticians who are dedicated to the task of conquering the "disease of crime." They must be given supreme command, undisputed authority, and the financial support needed to accomplish their mission.  Society must bow to superior scientific knowledge and reshape its own concepts and attitudes to conform to those voiced by qualified technicians in the scientific world.

Facetiously nothing would act as a greater deterrent to crime than for the criminal to be labeled "Incompetent" and to be regarded with the same benevolent tolerance associated with the mentally deformed or treated with the same careful consideration and pity. The word criminal has been glamorized and is subconsciously and erroneously associated with the words, heroic, tough, audacious and adventurous by the criminal himself. This is surely distorted thinking and in a sense may well be the only distinction he can claim. But to be regarded as mentally incompetent would be repulsive to him and would undoubtedly represent a severe blow to his self-esteem, which could tend to dissuade him from participating in further criminal pursuits.

With the present system, society benefits in several ways. The economy is stimulated which in turn creates more jobs, and the standard of living is elevated by the circulation of more money. People who might have been welfare recipients are provided with gainful employment along with a semblance of normality; and finally society is afforded some measure of protection from the criminal element. The last benefit is rather dubious; however, it is a fact that while there are approximately two million crimes committed annually, the prison population accounts for less than ten percent of the felons responsible for the commission of those crimes. It was just recently revealed that if all the jails and prisons were to be emptied simultaneously, there would be no appreciable rise in the crime rate; a fact which should give one considerable pause for thought. Aside from the humane and moralistic arguments put forth as reasons for condemnation of the system, a much stronger motivation must be advanced to induce change. One from which society must be convinced that its benefits will exceed those ascribed to the methods now being utilized.  With the exception of the eventual elimination of recidivism, the most profitable motive for instituting change can be found in the criminal himself.  The average criminal, is of above average intelligence, is creative, resourceful, talented, skilled and industrious.  His value to society, once he is habilitated and reformed, and he is able to conform to a normal pattern of behavior wherein all of his energies are channeled into a productive and creative course, becomes significant enough to warrant the effort needed to cultivate his reformation.  This portion of the population has a wealth of potential.  Intellectual and physical productivity is going unrecognized, untapped and wasted.

The nation today is experiencing the labor pains of a "renaissance".  People, especially the young, are beginning to strip away the embroidered raiment's of old, hitherto, undisputed doctrines.  Values, both moral and social, are being re-assessed, modified or discarded.  The democracy is being subjected to the severest of tests and inquisitions of its two hundred year history.  Its greatest strength has not come from the founding fathers, nor from the politico-militarists who organized the people, but from the people themselves, whose common bond was a militarists unquenchable thirst for liberty and justice for all.  The same pursuits provide the catalyst for the more civilized and better educated revolutionary of the "now" generation.

Perhaps the strongest point that can be made here is to observe that crime is but another symptom of a diseased eco-socio-politico-organism that has been kept under control all through the years by the simple expediency of treating the symptoms rather than going to the heart of the disease itself and destroying the bacteria that sustains it.  The word crime is defined as "an act committed or omitted in violation of a law." The criminal justice system is technically guilty of the crime of omission when it elects to mete out punishment for a criminal act without taking the initiative to eradicate the cause for crime. With all other facets of our society under attack, it is unreasonable to think that the criminal justice system can remain inviolate.

In this age when man's technological achievements have enabled him to conquer space and make exploratory forays to other planets, it is inconceivable to believe that he is incapable of mastering the problem of crime here in his native environment. If one can foresee the time when we must inevitably encounter intelligent life somewhere in the limitless vastness of outer space, the necessity to understand the thinking dynamics that control and regulate human behavior becomes a pressing priority. What better place to begin research than with a group of our own kind, whose thinking processes are clouded in mystery which continues to confound science. The criminal mind is a "k" factor in an equation yet to be pondered. We dream that it may be a means of opening the criminal mind to facilitate a candid view of his thinking apparatus and the effects of the system upon it.

No conscious effort has been made in this writing to dilute or disguise the bitterness, resentment, vindictiveness or animosity which clearly displays itself. However, the author has tried to confine his analysis to the boundaries of truth as perceived through an admittedly prejudiced and distorted lens. If it seems that rhetoric has been employed to dramatize the criminal's plight or to impress the reader, let this too weigh against the author and be given due consideration, but without prejudice to the issues or detracting from the constructive qualities of the critique.

"Are you a prisoner locked in a dark dungeon, for some petty offense, and condemned by those who wish to reform man by corrupting him." Kahlil Gibran

# APPENDIX 2

## DRAWINGS BY AL SAILER

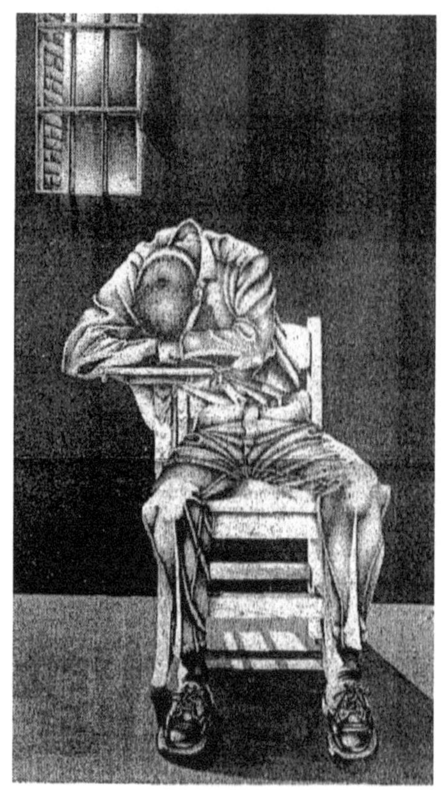

Alone

Search for Self

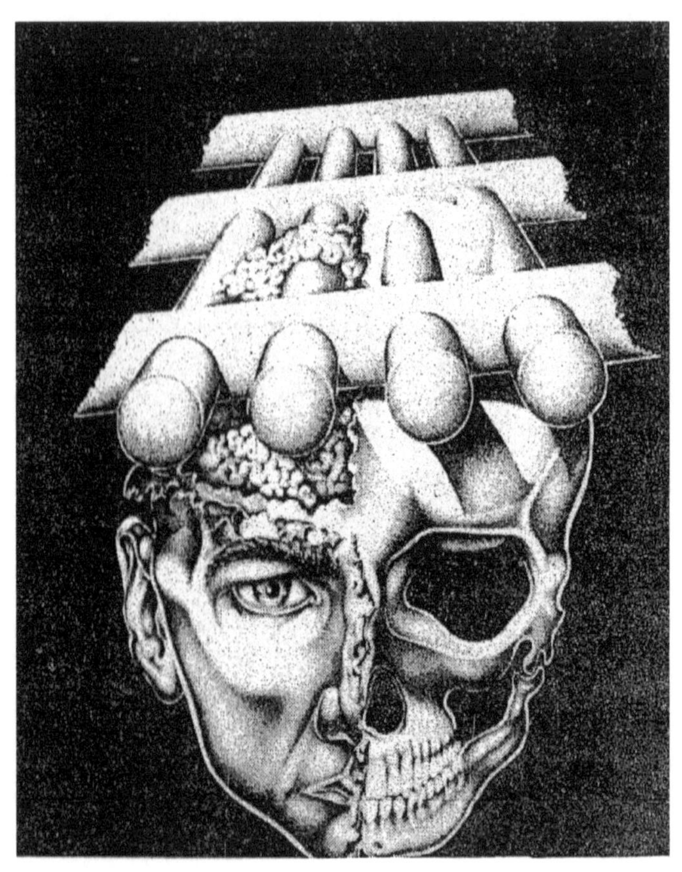

Untitled

# APPENDIX 3

Newspaper article published in Delaware County Daily Times
5-14-74

By Gerry Oliver
Daily Times Staff Writer

Broomall – Alfred Sailer of … Lawrence Park, has always liked to draw. But he never thought about it as a life's work when he dropped out of school in Wheeling, W. Va.

It was in the "cold grey world" of prison, where he's lived for 27 of the last 30 years, that he discovered his talent and developed it himself.

"I found the answer to my problems at my fingertips," he said. "Now I hope I can do something with it."

His parole officer, Joseph A. Marro who has been with the state federal parole offices for the last 20 years, has high hopes for Sailer.  He has been trying very hard to keep Sailer working creatively and to find an outlet for his talent.

"I took his 'grey period' work to the Pennsylvania Academy of Fine Arts and they were very impressed," Marro said: "They referred me to a major Philadelphia gallery, the Wall-Nuts, who are excited about giving Al a one-man show as soon as he adds a few pieces to the collection."

Marro, who spends his off-time as president of the Trilby String Band, of Philadelphia Mummers fame, doesn't consider himself an art specialist.  Nevertheless, he said:

"When Al first sent me a piece of his work, I was quite moved.  It can really get you."

What Sailer says of his art is that "It has taught me a lot of patience."

That's particularly true of his present style.  For the last few years he's been working primarily in pen and ink, doing some line work but largely a dot technique that's similar to hand-screening.  It has taken months of work, sometimes day and night, to complete each piece.

The result is boldly etched black and white work that is photographic in its precision but surrealistic in concept.

One of the first of his "grey period" works, entitled "The Weight of Time" was a gift to Marro.  It shows a severed hand holding a pocket watch with the suspended hand held fast by a huge block and tackle.

"I got the idea for the work when I was working in a steel mill," Sailer said.  It was one of the jobs he did during a work release program while he was serving time in Lewisburg Prison in Lewisburg, Pa.

On the back of most of his works he has written a short essay of explanation.

For "The Weight of Time," he has written:

"Time hangs heavy on every man and makes us all prisoners. . . The gory,
bleeding stump represents mortal being . . . The block and tackle, the solid durability in past mistakes and those yet to be made . . . The Watch, material reward.  All are tied directly to us . . . The unwrapped coil of steel represents the sentence I am now serving . . . the wrapper coil, the sentence served."

Prison became home to Sailer for more than half his life so far largely for passing worthless checks and forgeries.

"I was a very unsuccessful forger," Sailer quipped.  A soft-spoken medium-sized, athletically built man, he nevertheless still finds it hard to smile.

His personal problems began while he was in the U.S. Air Corps during World War II.  After several AWOL experiences, he was discharged in 1946 and 10 days later he wound up in jail.

Violence has had no part in his criminal record, Marro reported, but bitterness has.

"He has seen the inside of most federal and state penitentiaries between New York and Georgia," said Marro" "And he has served every inch of the time imposed on him so far.  He's never had any kind of break."

Right now, more than a month after coming to live with his mother, Mrs. Anna Sailer who is retired and living on Social Security, Sailer feels that much of his bitterness has dissipated.

Among his most recent works is a poster in color for the Trilby String Band, showing the dual nature of the bandsman – working man at one time and clowns another.

Marro also pointed out that Sailer has designed the special Trilby costumes for the 1976 Mummers Celebration. It's still "top secret," however. The poster will be reproduced in all types of promotional literature to be used by the band group.

Sailer has never had any professional instruction in art.

"I've taught myself and I've learned to work in all media," Sailer said.

Another big thing Sailer has done behind bars is read. "I've read everything from Jung to Overstreet and from St. Thomas to Erich Fromm." Sailer commented.

"He writes almost as well as he paints," Marro said. "In fact, he has written a critique on the penal system as he has seen it. But that's another story."

Most of his serious work in pen and ink has been done during the last half-dozen years, mostly at Lewisburg.

"When you spend a lot of time in prison, it's almost easier to go on living there than to come out," Sailer said. "It becomes kind of a haven, a way of life and lonely and meager as it is, you don't have to worry about the necessities of life – a place to sleep and food to eat."

Right now, Sailer is most interested in using his artistic creativity for gainful employment. He's been arranging for another smaller exhibition at the Ardmore Gallery and orienting himself to the world to which he has returned.

Today, at 52, Sailer is eager to build a new life.

"I'm feeling pretty good now about being home," he said.

www.ingramcontent.com/pod-product-compliance
Lightning Source LLC
Chambersburg PA
CBHW031256250726
48655CB00005B/2238